Contents

What do you think of this book? We want to hear from you!

Microsoft is interested in hearing your feedback so we can improve our books and learning resources for you. To participate in a brief survey, please visit:

https://aka.ms/tellpress

What do you think of this book? We want to hear from you!

Microsoft is interested in hearing your feedback so we can improve our books and learning resources for you. To participate in a brief survey, please visit:

https://aka.ms/tellpress

Introduction

The Microsoft Office Specialist (MOS) certification program has been designed to validate your knowledge of and ability to use programs in the Microsoft Office 2016 suite of programs. This book has been designed to guide you in studying the types of tasks you are likely to be required to demonstrate in Exam 77-731, "Outlook 2016: Core Communication, Collaboration and Email Skills."

Who this book is for

MOS 2016 Study Guide for Microsoft Outlook is designed for experienced computer users seeking Microsoft Office Specialist certification in Outlook 2016.

MOS exams for individual programs are practical rather than theoretical. You must demonstrate that you can complete certain tasks or projects rather than simply answer questions about program features. The successful MOS certification candidate will have at least six months of experience using all aspects of the program on a regular basis; for example, using Outlook at work or school to create and send messages, format message content, organize and manage messages, schedule appointments and events, manage meetings, store information in notes, track tasks, store contact information, locate information, and print and save information. You should also know how to customize Outlook settings and automate tasks within Outlook.

As a certification candidate, you probably have a lot of experience with the program you want to become certified in. Many of the procedures described in this book will be familiar to you; others might not be. Read through each study section and ensure that you are familiar with the procedures, concepts, and tools discussed. In some cases, images depict the tools you will use to perform procedures related to the skill set. Study the images and ensure that you are familiar with the options available for each tool.

> **See Also** The information in this book is focused specifically on skills required for Microsoft Office Specialist certification. For more expansive information about Outlook 2016, read *Microsoft Outlook 2016 Step by Step* by Joan Lambert (Microsoft Press, 2016). This 592-page book provides in-depth information about all aspects of the Outlook program and useful tips for increasing efficiency.

How this book is organized

The exam coverage is divided into chapters representing broad skill sets that correlate to the functional groups covered by the exam. Each chapter is divided into sections addressing groups of related skills that correlate to the exam objectives. Each section includes review information, generic procedures, and practice tasks you can complete on your own while studying. When necessary, practice files you can use to work through the practice tasks are provided. Because Outlook items such as messages and contact records are specific to the email account, you create those as you work through the practice tasks. You can practice the generic procedures in this book by using the supplied practice files or by using your own files.

Download the practice files

To copy the book's practice files to your computer, download the compressed (zipped) folder from the following page, and extract the files from it to a folder (such as your Documents folder) on your computer:

   https://aka.ms/MOSOutlook2016/downloads

IMPORTANT The Outlook 2016 program is not available from this website. You should purchase and install that program before using this book.

The following table lists the practice files provided for this book.

Folder and objective group	Practice files
MOSOutlook2016\Objective1 Manage the Outlook environment for productivity	None
MOSOutlook2016\Objective2 Manage messages	Outlook_2-2a.docx Outlook_2-2b.pptx Outlook_2-3.docx
MOSOutlook2016\Objective3 Manage schedules	Outlook_3-2.docx
MOSOutlook2016\Objective4 Manage contacts and groups	Outlook_4-1.png

Adapt procedure steps

This book contains many images of user interface elements that you'll work with while performing tasks in Outlook on a Windows computer. Depending on your screen resolution or program window width, the Outlook program or item window ribbon on your screen might look different from that shown in this book. (If you turn on Touch mode, the ribbon displays significantly fewer commands than in Mouse mode.) As a result, procedural instructions that involve the ribbon might require a little adaptation.

Simple procedural instructions use this format:

→ On the **Insert** tab, in the **Illustrations** group, click **Pictures**.

If the command is in a list, our instructions use this format:

→ On the **Home** tab, in the **Tags** group, click the **Follow Up** arrow, and then click **Today**.

If differences between your display settings and ours cause a button to appear differently on your screen than it does in this book, you can easily adapt the steps to locate the command. First click the specified tab, and then locate the specified group. If a group has been collapsed into a group list or under a group button, click the list or button to display the group's commands. If you can't immediately identify the button you want, point to likely candidates to display their names in ScreenTips.

The instructions in this book assume that you're interacting with on-screen elements on your computer by clicking (with a mouse, touchpad, or other hardware device). If you're using a different method—for example, if your computer has a touchscreen interface and you're tapping the screen (with your finger or a stylus)—substitute the applicable tapping action when you interact with a user interface element.

Instructions in this book refer to user interface elements that you click or tap on the screen as *buttons*, and to physical buttons that you press on a keyboard as *keys*, to conform to the standard terminology used in documentation for these products.

Ebook edition

If you're reading the ebook edition of this book, you can do the following:

- Search the full text
- Print
- Copy and paste

You can purchase and download the ebook edition from the Microsoft Press Store at:

https://aka.ms/MOSOutlook2016/detail

Errata, updates, & book support

We've made every effort to ensure the accuracy of this book and its companion content. If you discover an error, please submit it to us through the link at:

https://aka.ms/MOSOutlook2016/errata

If you need to contact the Microsoft Press Book Support team, please send an email message to:

mspinput@microsoft.com

For help with Microsoft software and hardware, go to:

https://support.microsoft.com

We want to hear from you

At Microsoft Press, your satisfaction is our top priority, and your feedback our most valuable asset. Please tell us what you think of this book by completing the survey at:

https://aka.ms/tellpress

The survey is short, and we read every one of your comments and ideas. Thanks in advance for your input!

Stay in touch

Let's keep the conversation going! We're on Twitter at:

https://twitter.com/MicrosoftPress

Taking a Microsoft Office Specialist exam

Desktop computing proficiency is increasingly important in today's business world. When screening, hiring, and training employees, employers can feel reassured by relying on the objectivity and consistency of technology certification to ensure the competence of their workforce. As an employee or job seeker, you can use technology certification to prove that you already have the skills you need to succeed, saving current and future employers the time and expense of training you.

Microsoft Office Specialist certification

Microsoft Office Specialist certification is designed to assist students and information workers in validating their skills with Office programs. The following certification paths are available:

- A Microsoft Office Specialist (MOS) is an individual who has demonstrated proficiency by passing a certification exam in one or more Office programs, including Microsoft Word, Excel, PowerPoint, Outlook, or Access.

- A Microsoft Office Specialist Expert (MOS Expert) is an individual who has taken his or her knowledge of Office to the next level and has demonstrated by passing Core and Expert certification exams that he or she has mastered the more advanced features of Word or Excel.

- A Microsoft Office Specialist Master (MOS Master) is an individual who has demonstrated a broader knowledge of Office skills by passing the Word Core and Expert exams, the Excel Core and Expert exams, the PowerPoint exam, and the Access or Outlook exam.

Selecting a certification path

When deciding which certifications you would like to pursue, assess the following:

- The program and program version(s) with which you are familiar
- The length of time you have used the program and how frequently you use it
- Whether you have had formal or informal training in the use of that program
- Whether you use most or all of the available program features
- Whether you are considered a go-to resource by business associates, friends, and family members who have difficulty with the program

Candidates for MOS certification are expected to successfully complete a wide range of standard business tasks. Successful candidates generally have six or more months of experience with the specific Office program, including either formal, instructor-led training or self-study using MOS-approved books, guides, or interactive computer-based materials.

Candidates for MOS Expert and MOS Master certification are expected to successfully complete more complex tasks that involve using the advanced functionality of the program. Successful candidates generally have at least six months, and might have several years, of experience with the programs, including formal, instructor-led training or self-study using MOS-approved materials.

Test-taking tips

Every MOS certification exam is developed from a set of exam skill standards (referred to as the *objective domain*) that are derived from studies of how the Office programs are used in the workplace. Because these skill standards dictate the scope of each exam, they provide critical information about how to prepare for certification. This book follows the structure of the published exam objectives.

> **See Also** For more information about the book structure, see "How this book is organized" in the Introduction.

The MOS certification exams are performance based and require you to complete business-related tasks in the program for which you are seeking certification. For example, you might be presented with a document and told to insert and format additional document elements. Your score on the exam reflects how many of the requested tasks you complete within the allotted time.

Here is some helpful information about taking the exam:

- Keep track of the time. Your exam time does not officially begin until after you finish reading the instructions provided at the beginning of the exam. During the exam, the amount of time remaining is shown in the exam instruction window. You can't pause the exam after you start it.

- Pace yourself. At the beginning of the exam, you will receive information about the tasks that are included in the exam. During the exam, the number of completed and remaining tasks is shown in the exam instruction window.

- Read the exam instructions carefully before beginning. Follow all the instructions provided completely and accurately.

- If you have difficulty performing a task, you can restart it without affecting the result of any completed tasks, or you can skip the task and come back to it after you finish the other tasks on the exam.

- Enter requested information as it appears in the instructions, but without duplicating the formatting unless you are specifically instructed to do so. For example, the text and values you are asked to enter might appear in the instructions in bold and underlined text, but you should enter the information without applying these formats.

- Close all dialog boxes before proceeding to the next exam item unless you are specifically instructed not to do so.

- Don't close task panes before proceeding to the next exam item unless you are specifically instructed to do so.

- If you are asked to print a document, worksheet, chart, report, or slide, perform the task, but be aware that nothing will actually be printed.

- Don't worry about extra keystrokes or mouse clicks. Your work is scored based on its result, not on the method you use to achieve that result (unless a specific method is indicated in the instructions).

- If a computer problem occurs during the exam (for example, if the exam does not respond or the mouse no longer functions) or if a power outage occurs, contact a testing center administrator immediately. The administrator will restart the computer and return the exam to the point where the interruption occurred, with your score intact.

Exam Strategy This book includes special tips for effectively studying for the Microsoft Office Specialist exams in Exam Strategy paragraphs such as this one.

Certification benefits

At the conclusion of the exam, you will receive a score report, indicating whether you passed the exam. If your score meets or exceeds the passing standard (the minimum required score), you will be contacted by email by the Microsoft Certification Program team. The email message you receive will include your Microsoft Certification ID and links to online resources, including the Microsoft Certified Professional site. On this site, you can download or order a printed certificate, create a virtual business card, order an ID card, review and share your certification transcript, access the Logo Builder, and access other useful and interesting resources, including special offers from Microsoft and affiliated companies.

Depending on the level of certification you achieve, you will qualify to display one of three logos on your business card and other personal promotional materials. These logos attest to the fact that you are proficient in the applications or cross-application skills necessary to achieve the certification. Using the Logo Builder, you can create a personalized certification logo that includes the MOS logo and the specific programs in which you have achieved certification. If you achieve MOS certification in multiple programs, you can include multiple certifications in one logo.

For more information

To learn more about the Microsoft Office Specialist exams and related courseware, visit:

http://www.certiport.com/mos

Microsoft Office Specialist

Exam 77-731

Outlook 2016: Core Communication, Collaboration and Email Skills

This book covers the skills you need to have for certification as a Microsoft Office Specialist in Outlook 2016. Specifically, you need to be able to complete tasks that demonstrate the following skill sets:

1. Manage the Outlook environment for productivity
2. Manage messages
3. Manage schedules
4. Manage contacts and groups

With these skills, you can efficiently manage communications with colleagues and perform the scheduling and tracking tasks that are important to working efficiently in a business environment.

Prerequisites

This book assumes that you have been working with Outlook 2016 for at least six months and that you know how to perform fundamental tasks that are not specifically mentioned in the objectives for this Microsoft Office Specialist exam. Before you begin studying for this exam, you might want to make sure you are familiar with the information in this section.

Work in individual modules

Mail module

Each time you start Outlook and connect to your email server, any new messages received since the last time you connected appear in your Inbox. Depending on your settings, Outlook downloads either the entire message to your computer or only the message header. The headers, which are listed in the content pane to the right of the Folder Pane, provide basic information about the message, such as:

- The item type (such as message, meeting request, or task assignment).
- The sender, recipient, and subject.
- The most recent response type.
- If it has attachments.
- If it has been digitally signed or encrypted.
- If it has been marked as being of high or low importance.

Messages you haven't yet read are indicated by vertical blue lines and bold headers. You can display the text of a message in these ways:

- You can open a message in its own window by double-clicking its header in the message list.
- You can read a message without opening it by clicking its header in the message list to display the message in the Reading Pane.

Calendar module

When you display the Calendar module, the Folder Pane changes to display the Date Navigator and a list of the local, Microsoft Exchange Server, Microsoft SharePoint, and Internet calendars that Outlook is configured to connect to.

People module

In the People module, the Folder Pane displays a list of the available address books. On the contact index to the right of the content pane in the People module, you can click alphabetic buttons to quickly jump to contact records filed by a specific letter.

Tasks and Notes modules

In the Tasks module, the Folder Pane displays the available task folders and task folder views. In the Notes module, it displays the available note folders.

Tip You can display the Mail, Calendar, People, Tasks, and Notes modules from the Navigation Bar at the bottom of the Folder Pane.

Switch views

You can use commands on the View tab of the ribbon to display different views of module content. If none of the standard views meets your needs, you can click the View Settings button in the Current View group on the View tab to define a custom view of the information in the current module.

Create Outlook items

You can create any type of Outlook item from any module. You can also create folders to contain items such as mail messages, calendar information, or contact records. You must specify the type of items the folder will contain when you create it.

To create an item specific to the current module

➔ On the **Home** tab, in the **New** group, click the **New *Item*** button.

➔ Press **Ctrl+N**.

Tip The New button always creates the default item for the current module. For example, in the Mail module, the New button and keyboard shortcut create a new message.

To create any item from any module

➜ On the **Home** tab, in the **New** group, click the **New Items** button, and then click the type of item you want to create.

➜ Press **Ctrl+Shift+M** to create a message.

➜ Press **Ctrl+Shift+A** to create an appointment.

➜ Press **Ctrl+Shift+Q** to create a meeting.

➜ Press **Ctrl+Shift+C** to create a contact.

➜ Press **Ctrl+Shift+L** to create a contact group.

➜ Press **Ctrl+Shift+K** to create a task.

➜ Press **Ctrl+Shift+N** to create a note.

To create a folder

1. Do either of the following to open the Create New Folder dialog box:

   • On the **Folder** tab, in the **New** group, click **New Folder**.

   • Press **Ctrl+Shift+E**.

2. In the **Name** box, enter a name for the folder.

3. In the **Folder contains** list, do one of the following:

   • To create a calendar, click **Calendar Items**.

   • To create an address book, click **Contact Items**.

   • To create an email folder, click **Mail and Post Items**.

   • To create a note folder, click **Note Items**.

   • To create a task list, click **Task Items**.

4. In the **Select where to place the folder** list, click the location in which you want to create the folder.

5. In the **Create New Folder** dialog box, click **OK**.

Address messages

To address an email message, enter the intended recipient's email address into the To box. If you want to send a message to more than one person, separate the addresses with semicolons. If a message recipient's address is in your address book, you can enter the person's name, and Outlook will look for the corresponding email address. (You can either wait for Outlook to validate the name or press Ctrl+K to immediately validate the names and addresses you enter.)

As you enter characters in the To, Cc, or Bcc box, Outlook might display matching addresses in a list below the box. Select a name or email address from the list and then press Tab or Enter to insert the entire name or address in the box.

If your email account is part of an Exchange Server network, you can send messages to another person on the same network by entering only his or her email alias (for example, if the full email address is *joan@wingtiptoys.com*, you need enter only *joan*)—the at symbol (@) and domain name aren't required.

By default, Outlook searches your Global Address List and main address book, but you can instruct the program to also search other address books. If no address book contains an entry for the name you entered, when you send the message, Outlook prompts you to select an address book entry or create a new contact.

To have Outlook search additional address books

1. On the **Home** tab, in the **Find** group, click **Address Book**.
2. In the **Address Book** window, on the **Tools** menu, click **Options**.
3. In the **Addressing** dialog box, click **Custom**, and then click **Add**.
4. In the **Add Address List** dialog box, click the address list you want to add, click **Add**, and then click **Close**.
5. In the **Addressing** dialog box, click **OK**, and then close the **Address Book** window.

Access program commands and options

You display the Backstage view by clicking the File tab on the ribbon. Commands for working with email accounts and Outlook items (rather than item content) are available from the Backstage view. You display the Backstage view by clicking the File tab on the ribbon in the Outlook program window or any Outlook item. When you display the Backstage view from the Outlook program window, the commands relate to the current account, current module, and selected item. The available commands vary based on the type of account selected in the account list at the top of the page.

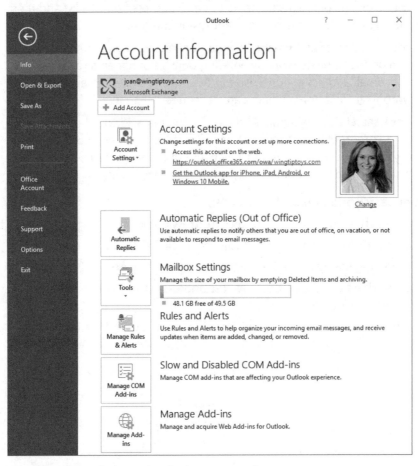

The Backstage view displays options for the current email account

The links in the left pane of the Backstage view provide access to pages of commands for working with the current email account, commands for working with the active Outlook item, or commands for working with Outlook. To display the Info, Open & Export, Save As, Print, Office Account, Feedback, or Support page, click the page name in the left pane.

You manage many aspects of Outlook functionality from the Outlook Options dialog box, which you open by clicking Options in the left pane of the Backstage view.

The Outlook Options dialog box

The Outlook Options dialog box has 12 separate pages of commands (13 for Microsoft Exchange Server accounts), organized by function. To display the General, Mail, Calendar, Groups, People, Tasks, Search, Language, Advanced, Customize Ribbon, Quick Access Toolbar, Add-ins, or Trust Center page of the Outlook Options dialog box, click the page name in the left pane.

To save changes that you make in the Outlook Options dialog box, click OK in the lower-right corner. To discard changes, click Cancel.

Objective group 1
Manage the Outlook environment for productivity

The skills tested in this section of the Microsoft Office Specialist exam for Microsoft Outlook 2016 relate to managing the Outlook environment. Specifically, the following objectives are associated with this set of skills:

1.1 Customize settings

1.2 Print and save information

1.3 Perform search operations in Outlook

The goal of the Office 2016 working environment is to make working with content, including that of Microsoft Word documents, Excel workbooks, PowerPoint presentations, Outlook email messages, and Access database tables, as intuitive as possible. To that end, each program in the Office system, including Outlook, has a similar user interface.

Unlike other Office programs, Outlook doesn't function for a single purpose or create a single category of files. You use it to create, organize, and track several types of information that are critical to keeping your daily life functioning smoothly. To minimize the work of dealing with such diverse items of information as email messages, contact records, appointments, tasks, and notes, Outlook provides a module for each type and presents each module in a similar interface, making it possible for you to work with different items in consistent ways.

This chapter guides you in studying ways of customizing your Outlook installation and settings to fit the way you work, and performing operations such as printing, saving, and searching that are common across all Outlook modules.

> No practice files are required to complete the practice tasks in this chapter. For more information, see "Download the practice files" in this book's introduction.

Objective 1.1: Customize settings

Manage multiple accounts

You can add one or more email accounts of any supported type to your Outlook profile, either during the initial setup procedure or at any time thereafter. After you configure Outlook to connect to an email account, you can easily manage the information stored with that account by using the Outlook features specifically designed for each type of information.

Configuring Outlook creates an Outlook data file for each email account and an Outlook profile, which stores information about you and your email accounts. You can work with your profile from within Outlook or from the Mail control panel in Windows. Your profile includes information about your email account such as the user name, display name, server name, password, and the local data storage location. You can connect to more than one email account per profile, to seamlessly manage all your email communications through Outlook.

> **Exam Strategy** Exam 77-731, "Outlook 2016: Core Communication, Collaboration and Email Skills," does not require you to demonstrate the ability to work with Outlook profiles.

If you configure Outlook to connect to multiple email accounts, or if you have been delegated control of another account, you need to ensure that Outlook sends outgoing messages from the correct account. By default, Outlook assumes that you intend to send a message from the account you're currently working in. If you begin composing a message while viewing the Inbox of your work account, for example, Outlook selects the work account as the message-sending account. If you reply to a message received by your personal account, Outlook selects the personal account as the message-sending account. You can change the sending account from within the message composition window.

> **See Also** For information about delegating account access, see "Delegate access" in "Objective 2.4: Organize and manage messages."

Outlook displays the account folders for each mailbox in the Folder Pane. You manage settings for each account separately, but Outlook tracks flagged items and calendar items for all accounts (other than secondary Microsoft Exchange accounts) in your primary Task List and Calendar.

> **Exam Strategy** You can connect Outlook to email accounts that support automatic connection and to email accounts that require you to manually enter server information. Exam 77-731, "Outlook 2016: Core Communication, Collaboration and Email Skills," may require you to demonstrate the ability to add an email account to an existing Outlook configuration. You will not be required to demonstrate the process of setting up Outlook from a clean installation.

To start the email account connection process from within Outlook

→ On the **Info** page of the Backstage view, click the **Add Account** button to display the Auto Account Setup page of the Add Account wizard.

To connect to an email account that supports automatic connections

1. Display the **Auto Account Setup** page of the **Add Account** wizard.

2. Enter your name, email address, and email account password in the text boxes provided. Then click **Next** to search your available networks and the Internet for the specified domain.

Tip The password characters you enter are hidden, so take care that the Caps Lock key is not inadvertently active when you enter the password.

If the wizard locates an account matching the specified email address, it attempts to log on by using the password you provided. If the connection isn't immediately successful, Outlook displays a dialog box and prompts you for the user name and password. If the connection is successful, a confirmation appears, along with additional account configuration options.

Tip Outlook may prompt you to reenter the user name and password even if you entered it correctly the first time.

Add Account	✕
Congratulations!	

Configuring

Outlook is completing the setup for your account. This might take several minutes.

✓ Establishing network connection
✓ **Searching for joan@wingtiptoys.com settings**
✓ Logging on to the mail server

Congratulations! Your email account was successfully configured and is ready to use.

☐ Change account settings   Add another account...

< Back   **Finish**   Cancel

You can begin using the account now, or connect to additional accounts

3. Do either of the following:

   • Click **Finish** to start using the account.

   • Click **Add another account** to restart the wizard.

To connect manually to an email account

1. Display the **Auto Account Setup** page of the **Add Account** wizard, select **Manual setup or additional server types**, and then click **Next**.

Connection processes vary by account type

2. On the **Choose Your Account Type** page, do either of the following:

    *   Select **Office 365**, enter your Office 365 account email address, and then click **Next**.

    *   Select **POP or IMAP** or **Exchange ActiveSync**, and then click **Next** to display the Account Settings page for that type of account.

3. Follow the wizard's prompts to provide necessary information and complete the setup process. The level of information required varies based on the account type.

Settings for a POP account

Tip In this procedure, the images depict the settings for a POP account. The process of completing the wizard is similar for IMAP accounts. Less information is required for Exchange ActiveSync accounts.

---

4. When configuring a POP or IMAP account, click the **More Settings** button to open the Internet Email Settings dialog box in which you can enter additional information, such as the name by which you want to identify the account, the email address you want to appear when you reply to a message, and outgoing server authentication information. Review the settings on each tab and configure any that are necessary. Then click **OK** to close the dialog box and return to the Account Settings page.

5. On the **Account Settings** page, click **Next** to test the connection.

Test Account Settings

Congratulations! All tests completed successfully. Click Close to continue.

Stop

Close

Tasks   Errors

Tasks	Status
✓ Log onto incoming mail server (POP3)	Completed
✓ Send test email message	Completed

Testing confirms that you can send and receive messages with the current settings

6. Close the **Test Account Settings** dialog box, and then click **Finish** to start using the account.

To manage settings for a specific account

→ In the account list at the top of the **Info** page of the Backstage view, select the account you want to manage.

To specify the sending account for a message, invitation, or assignment

→ To send from an account that is configured in Outlook, click the **From** button in the message header, and then click the account from which you want to send the message.

☐ ↑ ↓ ✕ ⩴   Untitled - Message (HTML)   ⊞ — ☐ ✕

File   Message   Insert   Options   Format Text   Review   ♀ Tell me what you want to do

From ▼   Wingtip Toys

joan@otsi.com

Send   Personal

Wingtip Toys

Other Email Address...

The From button appears only if you have Outlook configured to connect to multiple accounts

→ To send from an account that is not configured in Outlook, click the **From** button in the message header, and then click **Other Email Address**. In the **Send From Other Email Address** dialog box, enter the account from which you want to send the message in the **From** box, select an installed account that has permission to send as that account, and then click **OK**.

Send from any account you have permissions for

Customize the appearance of the program window

You can control the display, and in some cases the location, of program window elements from the View tab of each module. In addition to the title bar, ribbon, and status bar that are common to all Office programs, the Outlook program window includes four areas in which you work with Outlook items.

Primary areas of the Outlook program window

The four content areas of the Outlook program window are as follows:

- **Folder Pane** This collapsible pane appears on the left side of the Outlook program window in every module. Its contents change depending on the module you're viewing—it might display links to email folders, Microsoft SharePoint lists and libraries, external content, or view options. The Folder Pane state (minimized or expanded) remains the same as you switch among modules.

  When the compact Navigation Bar is displayed, it is incorporated into the Folder Pane and displayed vertically when the Folder Pane is minimized or horizontally when the Folder Pane is open.

- **Content pane** The content pane is the part of the program window bordered on the left by the Folder Pane and on the right by the To-Do Bar when the To-Do Bar is displayed, or by the right side of the program window when it is not displayed. The content pane displays the content of the selected module—your message list, calendar, contact records, or tasks.

- **Reading Pane** This optional pane can be displayed vertically to the right of the content pane or horizontally below it. Within the Reading Pane, you can preview and work with the content of a selected item, or display a full-featured preview of a file that is attached to an Outlook item (including Microsoft Word documents, Excel worksheets, PowerPoint presentations, and PDF files). The Reading Pane can also host the People Pane.

  Exam Strategy Exam 77-731, "Outlook 2016: Core Communication, Collaboration and Email Skills," does not require that you demonstrate the ability to work with the People Pane. For that reason, this Study Guide doesn't include information or procedures related to the People Pane.

  The Reading Pane can be displayed in any Outlook module but is displayed by default only in the Mail and Tasks modules.

- **To-Do Bar** This optional pane can display a monthly calendar, upcoming appointments, favorite contacts, and your task list, or any combination of these that you choose. In Outlook 2016, the To-Do Bar can be either open or closed, but not minimized as it could be in previous versions of Outlook.

  The To-Do Bar can be displayed in any Outlook module, but is not displayed by default in any module.

The Navigation Bar is located near the lower-left corner of the program window, above the status bar. In versions of Outlook before Outlook 2013, the navigation controls were incorporated into the Folder Pane (formerly called the Navigation Pane). In Outlook 2016, the navigation controls are presented on the Navigation Bar, which can appear as a compact vertical or horizontal bar that displays only module icons, or as a larger horizontal bar with text labels.

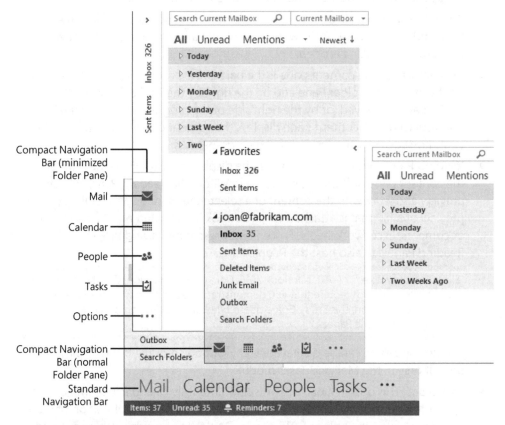

The Navigation Bar has multiple configurations

You can display the Mail, Calendar, People, and Tasks modules by clicking the corresponding button on the Navigation Bar. If a module name doesn't appear on the Navigation Bar, click the ellipsis at the right end of the Navigation Bar, and then click the module name to display it.

You can "peek" at the current content of the Calendar, People, or Tasks module by pointing to the module button. *Peeks* display information that in previous versions of Outlook was shown only on the To-Do Bar. The Calendar peek displays this month's Date Navigator and today's appointments, the People peek displays the contacts you've saved as favorites and a search box, and the Tasks peek displays your upcoming tasks and a task entry box. Docking a peek creates an area on the right side of the program window, called the To-Do Bar.

The Tasks peek (undocked)

Tip If the To-Do Bar isn't already open, pinning a peek displays it. Peeks are displayed on the To-Do Bar in the order that you add them. To change the order, remove all peeks other than the one you want on top, and then select other peeks in the order you want them. You configure the To-Do Bar content and presence separately for each module.

You can change the appearance of the Navigation Bar and the module buttons that it displays from the Navigation Options dialog box.

Configure the Navigation Bar appearance and functionality

The compact Navigation Bar is incorporated into the Folder Pane and its orientation depends on whether the Folder Pane is minimized or expanded. The standard Navigation Bar is separate from the Folder Pane and does not change orientation. To display more or fewer buttons on the standard Navigation Bar, modify the settings in the Navigation Options dialog box.

To display or close the Folder Pane

→ On the **View** tab, in the **Layout** group, click the **Folder Pane** button, and then click **Normal** to display the pane or **Off** to hide it.

To minimize or expand the Folder Pane

→ On the **View** tab, in the **Layout** group, click the **Folder Pane** button, and then click **Minimized**.

→ At the top of the **Folder Pane**, click the **Minimize the Folder Pane** button or the **Click to expand Folder Pane** button.

To change the width of the Folder Pane or To-Do Bar

→ Drag the divider between the **Folder Pane** or **To-Do Bar** and the content pane to the right or left.

To switch between the compact and standard Navigation Bar

1. On the **Navigation Bar**, click the ellipsis, and then click **Navigation Options**.
2. In the **Navigation Options** dialog box, select or clear the **Compact Navigation** check box, and then click **OK**.

To change the number of buttons on the Navigation Bar

➜ To display more or fewer buttons on the vertical (minimized) compact Navigation Bar, point to its top border, and when the pointer changes to a double-headed arrow, drag the border up or down.

➜ To display more or fewer buttons on the horizontal compact Navigation Bar, change the width of the Folder Pane.

Or

1. On the **Navigation Bar**, click the ellipsis, and then click **Navigation Options**.

2. In the **Navigation Options** dialog box, set the maximum number of visible items (you can display up to eight), and then click **OK**.

To change the order of buttons on the Navigation Bar

➜ In the **Navigation Options** dialog box, move module names up and down in the **Display in this order** box to set the order of the module buttons from left to right on the Navigation Bar.

To display peeks

➜ On the **Navigation Bar**, point to (don't click) the **Calendar**, **People**, or **Tasks** button or link.

To dock peeks to the To-Do Bar

➜ Do either of the following:

● Display the peek that you want to add to the To-Do Bar. In the upper-right corner of the peek, click the **Dock the peek** button.

● On the **View** tab, in the **Layout** group, click the **To-Do Bar** button, and then click any inactive peek (without a check mark) to pin it to the To-Do Bar.

To remove peeks from the To-Do Bar

➜ On the **To-Do Bar**, in the upper-right corner of the peek, click the **Remove the peek** button (the **X**).

➜ On the **View** tab, in the **Layout** group, click the **To-Do Bar** button, and then click any active peek to remove it from the To-Do Bar.

To hide the To-Do Bar in the active module

➜ On the **View** tab, in the **Layout** group, click the **To-Do Bar** button, and then click **Off**.

To resize the To-Do Bar or its content

➜ To change the width of the To-Do Bar, point to the left edge of the To-Do Bar, and when the pointer turns into a double-headed arrow, drag to the left or right.

➜ To change the height of a peek, point to the separator between two peeks, and when the pointer changes to a double-headed arrow, drag up or down.

Configure program options

You can change many of the default program settings from the Outlook Options dialog box. From this dialog box, you can control the settings and appearance of many Outlook features, including the following:

- Email accounts, functionality, and formatting
- Editorial and archive functions
- The Folder Pane and Reading Pane
- Your calendar, task list, and address books
- The indexing and search functions
- Message flagging
- The content of the Quick Access Toolbar and ribbon

The Outlook Options dialog box is divided into eight pages of function-specific settings (nine for Exchange accounts), two pages of feature-specific settings (for the ribbon and for the Quick Access Toolbar), and two pages of security-related settings.

Options for replying to, forwarding, and saving messages

Exam Strategy The Groups page is present only for Exchange accounts. Exam 77-731, "Outlook 2016: Core Communication, Collaboration and Email Skills," does not require you to demonstrate your ability to work with groups of this type.

Tip The Microsoft Office Specialist exam for Outlook 2016 includes objectives related to specific settings that are documented individually in this book. However, the Outlook Options dialog box contains other options not included on the exam, which are not covered in this book. Be sure to look through the Outlook Options dialog box for options that you could reconfigure to increase your efficiency while working in Outlook.

To specify the default format of outgoing messages

1. Open the **Outlook Options** dialog box and display the **Mail** page.
2. In the **Compose messages** section, in the **Compose messages in this format** list, click **HTML**, **Rich Text Format**, or **Plain Text**.
3. In the **Outlook Options** dialog box, click **OK** to save the changes.

To specify the text included in response messages

1. Open the **Outlook Options** dialog box and display the **Mail** page.
2. In the **Replies and forwards** section, click the message options you want for original content that is included in response messages, in the **When replying to a message** and **When forwarding a message** lists.
3. In the **Outlook Options** dialog box, click **OK** to save the changes.

To insert an identifier before inline responses

1. Do either of the following:
    *   On the **Personal Stationery** tab of the **Signatures and Stationery** dialog box, in the **Replying or forwarding messages** area, select the **Mark my comments with** check box.
    *   On the **Mail** page of the **Outlook Options** dialog box, in the **Replies and forwards** section, select the **Preface comments with** check box.
2. In the corresponding text box, enter the text that will identify your responses.
3. In the open dialog box, click **OK** to save the changes.

To have Outlook set the color of response text

→ On the **Personal Stationery** tab of the **Signatures and Stationery** dialog box, in the **Replying or forwarding messages** area, select the **Pick a new color when replying or forwarding** check box.

Objective 1.1 practice tasks

There are no practice files for these tasks.

➤ Start Outlook and do the following:

❑ Display the standard (not compact) Navigation Bar. Configure it to display links to only the People, Calendar, and Mail modules, in that order.

❑ Display and then dock the Calendar peek.

❑ Minimize the Folder Pane.

❑ Configure Outlook to compose outgoing messages in HTML.

❑ Configure Outlook to insert your initials between asterisks (for example, *JL*) before comments that you insert in message responses.

Objective 1.2: Print and save information

View and save messages and attachments

You can view message attachments in several ways:

- You can preview certain types of attachments (including Word documents, Excel workbooks, PowerPoint presentations, PDF files, and many types of image files) directly in the Reading Pane.

  When you click the attachment, the message text is replaced by a preview of the attachment contents, and the Attachments tool tab appears on the ribbon.

You can quickly preview many types of attachments in the Reading Pane

- You can open the attachment in the program assigned to that file type.

- You can save the attachment to your hard disk and open it from there. This strategy is recommended if you suspect an attachment might contain a virus because you can scan the file for viruses before opening it (provided that you have a virus scanning program installed and turned on).

If you want to save messages outside of Outlook, you can save either individual messages or entire folders of messages. Individual messages can be saved in several formats, including as Outlook message files, text files, and HTML files. Folders can be saved as Outlook data files, which can then be opened from any Outlook installation.

To preview message attachments

→ In the **Reading Pane**, do the following:

    a. To replace the message text with the attachment content, click the attachment (one time) in the message header.

    b. To redisplay the message content, click the **Back to message** button in the upper-left corner of the Reading Pane.

To open message attachments

→ In the **Reading Pane** or in an open message window, double-click the attachment in the message header.

To save message attachments to Outlook

→ To add a contact record or business card to your primary address book, drag the attachment from the email message to the **Contacts** button on the **Navigation Bar**.

→ To add a contact record or business card to a secondary address book, display the address book in the **Folder Pane**, and then drag the attachment to that folder.

To save message attachments to a file storage location

1. Open the **Save All Attachments** dialog box by doing any of the following:

    • Right-click any attachment, and then click **Save All Attachments**.

    • In the message header, click a message attachment. Then on the **Attachments** tool tab, click the **Save All Attachments** button.

    • In the left pane of the Backstage view, click **Save Attachments**.

2. In the **Save All Attachments** dialog box, select the attachments you want to save, and then click **OK**.

3. In the **Save Attachment** dialog box, browse to the folder in which you want to save the files, and then click **OK**.

To save messages as files

1. In the Backstage view of the message reading window, click **Save As**.
2. In the **Save As** dialog box, browse to the folder in which you want to save the message.
3. In the **Save as type** list, click the format in which you want to save the message.
4. If you want to change the name of the message file, replace the message subject in the **File name** box.
5. In the **Save As** dialog box, click **Save**.

To export messages to an Outlook data file

1. On the **Open & Export** page of the Backstage view, click **Import/Export** to start the Import And Export Wizard.
2. In the **Choose an action to perform** list, click **Export to a file**, and then click **Next**.
3. In the **Create a file of type** list, click **Outlook Data File (.pst)**, and then click **Next**.
4. In the **Select the folder to export from** list, click the folder from which you want to export messages.
5. If you want to export only some of the messages from the folder, click **Filter** to open the **Filter** dialog box, filter the folder to display only the messages you want to export, and then click **OK**.
6. In the **Export Outlook Data File** wizard, click **Next**.
7. To the right of the **Save exported file as** box, click the **Browse** button. In the **Open Outlook Data Files** dialog box, browse to the folder in which you want to save the .pst file. Enter a name for the exported file in the **File name** box, click **OK**, and then click **Next**.

Tip If other data files exist in the Open Outlook Data Files dialog box, the File Name box will automatically display the name of an existing file. You must replace that file name or the previous file will be overwritten.

---

8. On the wizard's last page, click **Finish**.
9. In the **Create Outlook Data File** dialog box, if you want to password-protect the file, enter a password in the **Password** and **Verify Password** boxes. Then click **OK** to create the file.

Print Outlook items

You can print any Outlook item from the content pane or from the item window.

You can print a list of the email messages in your Inbox or print one or more individual email messages. Outlook prints the message as shown on the screen, including font and paragraph formats. You can add information such as page headers and footers.

When printing a calendar, the amount of detail that appears depends on the time period you print and the print style you choose.

The Tri-fold calendar print style displays calendar items and tasks for the selected time period

Outlook offers several built-in print styles for calendars, and you can create others if you want. The available print styles vary based on what view you're in when you choose the Print command. The default print styles include:

- **Daily Style** Prints the selected date range with one day per page. Printed elements include the date, day, TaskPad, reference calendar for the current month, and an area for notes.

- **Weekly Agenda Style** Prints the selected date range with one calendar week per page, including reference calendars for the selected and following month.

- **Weekly Calendar Style** Prints the selected date range with one calendar week per page. Each page includes date range and time increments, reference calendars for the selected and following month, and TaskPad.

- **Monthly Style** Prints a page for each month in the selected date range. Each page includes the selected month with a few days showing from the previous and subsequent months, along with reference calendars for the selected and following month.

- **Tri-fold Style** Prints a page for each day in the selected date range. Each page includes the daily schedule, weekly schedule, and TaskPad.

- **Calendar Details Style** Lists your appointments for the selected date range, in addition to the accompanying appointment details.

You can select the date or range of dates to be printed and modify the page setup options to fit your needs.

You can print an address book or individual contact records, either on paper or to an electronic file (such as a PDF file or an XPS file), from any address book view.

Phone Directory Style prints only names and telephone numbers

Depending on the view, Outlook offers a variety of print styles, such as those described in the following table.

Style	Description	Available in views
Card	Contact information displayed alphabetically in two columns. Letter graphics appear at the top of each page and the beginning of each letter group.	Business Card, Card, People
Small Booklet	Contact information displayed alphabetically in one column. Formatted to print eight numbered pages per sheet. Letter graphics appear at the top of each page and the beginning of each letter group, and a contact index at the side of each page indicates the position of that page's entries in the alphabet.	Business Card, Card, People
Medium Booklet	Contact information displayed alphabetically in one column. Formatted to print four numbered pages per sheet. Letter graphics appear at the top of each page and the beginning of each letter group, and a contact index at the side of each page indicates the position of that page's entries in the alphabet.	Business Card, Card, People
Memo	Contact information displayed under a memo-like header that contains your name. One record per sheet.	Business Card, Card, People
Phone Directory	Contact names and phone numbers displayed in two columns. Letter graphics appear at the top of each page and the beginning of each letter group.	Business Card, Card, People
Table	Contact information displayed in a table that matches the on-screen layout.	Phone, List

You can customize the layout of most of the default print styles, and save the modified print styles.

To print the default view of an individual item

→ Right-click the item, and then click **Quick Print**.

To print an individual item

1. In the item window, display the **Print** page of the Backstage view.
2. Specify the print options and settings you want, and then click the **Print** button.

To print multiple items

1. In the content pane, select the items you want to print.
2. On the **Print** page of the Backstage view, specify the print options and settings you want, and then click **Print**.

To print a list view of all messages in a folder

→ On the **Print** page of the program window Backstage view, in the **Settings** section, click **Table Style**, and then click the **Print** button.

To print an email message and its attachments

1. On the **Print** page of the Backstage view, click the **Print Options** button.
2. In the **Print** dialog box, select the **Print attached files** check box. Then click **Print**.

To print a message attachment

1. In the **Reading Pane** or message window, select the attachments you want to print.
2. On the **Attachments** tool tab, in the **Actions** group, click the **Quick Print** button.

To print a calendar

1. In the Calendar module, on the **Print** page of the Backstage view, click the **Print Options** button.
2. In the **Print** dialog box, do the following:
   a. In the **Print style** list, click the print style you want.
   b. In the **Print range** section, specify the date range you want to print.
   c. If you want to exclude private appointments from the printed calendar, select the **Hide details of private appointments** check box.
3. In the **Print** dialog box, click the **Preview** button.
4. On the **Print** page of the Backstage view, click the **Print** button.

To print multiple contact records

1. In the People module, if you want to print only specific contact records, select those contact records.
2. On the **Print** page of the Backstage view, click the **Print Options** button.
3. In the **Print** dialog box, do the following:
   a. In the **Print style** list, click the print style you want.
   b. In the **Print range** section, click **All items** or **Only selected items**.
4. In the **Print** dialog box, click the **Preview** button.
5. On the **Print** page of the Backstage view, click the **Print** button.

To print tasks

1. In the Tasks module, if you want to print only specific task items and flagged items, select those items.
2. On the **Print** page of the Backstage view, click the **Print Options** button.
3. In the **Print** dialog box, do the following:
   a. In the **Print style** list, click the print style you want.
   b. In the **Print options** section, if you want to print files that are attached to the task items or flagged items, select the **Print attached files** check box.
4. In the **Print** dialog box, click the **Preview** button.
5. On the **Print** page of the Backstage view, click the **Print** button.

Objective 1.2 practice tasks

There are no practice files for these tasks. Save the results of the tasks in the **MOSOutlook2016\Objective1** practice file folder.

➤ Display your Inbox and do the following:

- ❑ Select two email messages that have attachments.
- ❑ In one operation, print both messages and their attachments.
- ❑ Save one of the messages to the practice file folder.
- ❑ Save the attachment only from the other message to the practice file folder.
- ❑ Export the content of your Inbox to an Outlook data file named <u>MyInbox</u>. Save the data file in the practice file folder.

➤ Display your default calendar and do the following:

- ❑ Print your calendar for the next three days so that the daily schedule for each day appears on its own page with space for a task list.

➤ Display your primary address book and do the following:

- ❑ Select four contact records.
- ❑ Print a list of the names and phone numbers.

➤ Display your task list and do the following:

- ❑ Print a table-style list of all your current tasks.

Objective 1.3:
Perform search operations in Outlook

Search for items

The Instant Search feature of Outlook 2016 makes it easy to find a specific Outlook item based on any text within the item or any attribute, such as the category assigned to it. With this very powerful search engine, you can find any message containing a specified search term, whether the term appears in the item header, in the item content, or in a message attachment.

Although you can use Instant Search to locate calendar items, contact records, and tasks, you will most often use it to locate messages in your Inbox and other mail folders. Regardless of the module you're searching from, you can search a specific folder, all folders containing items of that type, or all of Outlook. As you enter a search term, Outlook filters out all messages that don't match, displays only those items containing the characters you enter, and highlights the search term in the displayed results, making it easy to find exactly what you're looking for.

Outlook first displays up to 30 recent results. Clicking the More link at the bottom of the list or the Include Older Results button in the Results group on the Search tool tab displays additional results within the selected search scope. In the lower-left corner of the program window, the status bar displays the number of items included in the search results.

You can narrow the results by expanding the search term or by specifying other search criteria, such as the sender, the recipient (whether the message was addressed or only copied to you), a category assigned to the item, or whether the message contains attachments.

The Search tool tab appears when you activate the Search box in any Outlook module. You can enter search terms into the Search box and refine your search by using the commands on the Search tool tab.

You can refine a search by specifying item property values or value ranges

When searching any folder, you can use the commands on the Search tool tab to set the scope of the search and to more closely define the search specifications. You can also return to the results of previous searches.

The buttons available in the Scope and Refine groups vary based on the type of folder you're searching. The Scope group always offers the options of the current folder, all subfolders, all folders of the current type, and all Outlook items. The commands in the Refine group change to reflect common properties of items stored in the current folder type. The most common properties are shown as buttons in the Refine group; additional properties are available for selection from the More list.

Unless you specify otherwise, the search results include only the contents of the displayed folder, not any of its subfolders or any other folders. However, you can choose to search all similar folders or all Outlook items. If you search more than one folder, Outlook displays the search results grouped by the folder in which they appear.

You can open, delete, and process an item from the search results as you would from any other location. However, if you change an item so that it no longer fits the search criteria, the item no longer appears in the search results.

To search Outlook items in a specific folder

1. In the **Search** box at the top of the content pane, enter the search term.
2. On the **Search** tool tab, in the **Refine** group, click buttons to specify additional search criteria.

To change the scope of the search operation

→ To search all items in the current type of folder across all installed accounts, do either of the following:

- On the **Search** tool tab, in the **Scope** group, click the **All Items** button for the type of item contained in the current folder (for example, **All Mailboxes** or **All Calendar Items**).
- Press **Ctrl+Alt+A**.

→ To include subfolders of the current folder in the search, do either of the following:

- On the **Search** tool tab, in the **Scope** group, click the **Subfolders** button.
- Press **Ctrl+Alt+Z**.

→ To include messages, appointments, contact records, tasks, and notes from all installed accounts in the search, on the **Search** tool tab, in the **Scope** group, click the **All Outlook Items** button.

Tip The All Items and All Outlook Items searches include all accounts configured in your Outlook installation.

To return to the original content view

→ On the **Search** tool tab, in the **Close** group, click the **Close Search** button.
→ Click any folder in the **Folder Pane**.

To quickly return to previous search results

1. Click in the **Search** box at the top of the content pane to display the **Search** tool tab.

2. On the **Search** tool tab, in the **Options** group, click the **Recent Searches** button, and then click the search you want to repeat.

Use Search Folders

A Search Folder displays all the messages in your mailbox that match a specific set of search criteria, no matter which folders the messages are actually stored in. When you create a Search Folder, it becomes part of your mailbox and is kept up to date. The Search Folder module is located in the Folder Pane, within your top-level mailbox, at the same level as the Inbox.

By default, Outlook 2016 includes one standard Search Folder: Unread Mail. (If your environment includes Microsoft Skype for Business, you might also have Search Folders for Missed Calls and Missed Conversations.) If you want quick access to messages that fit a specific set of criteria, you can create a custom Search Folder. Search Folder categories include Reading Mail, Mail From People And Lists, Organizing Mail, and Custom.

New Search Folder	×
Select a Search Folder:	
Reading Mail	
Unread mail	
Mail flagged for follow up	
Mail either unread or flagged for follow up	
Important mail	
Mail from People and Lists	
Mail from and to specific people	
Mail from specific people	
Mail sent directly to me	
Mail sent to public groups	
Organizing Mail	
Categorized mail	
Large mail	
Old mail	
Mail with attachments	
Mail with specific words	
Custom	
Create a custom Search Folder	

Quickly create a standard Search Folder, or specify custom properties

Outlook automatically keeps Search Folder contents up to date. The names of folders containing unread or flagged items are bold, with the number of unread items after the folder name. The names of folders whose contents are not up to date are italic.

Each message in your mailbox is stored in only one folder (such as your Inbox), but it might appear in multiple Search Folders. Changing or deleting a message in a Search Folder changes or deletes the message in the folder in which it is stored.

To create Search Folders

1. Display any mail folder.
2. Do one of the following:
   - On the **Folder** tab, in the **New** group, click **New Search Folder** to open the **New Search Folder** dialog box.
   - In the **Folder Pane**, expand the mailbox for which you want to create the Search Folder, right-click **Search Folders**, and then click **New Search Folder**.
   - Press **Ctrl+Shift+P**.
3. In the **New Search Folder** dialog box, click the type of Search Folder you want to create, provide the search criteria that define the Search Folder contents, and then click **OK**.

To modify criteria for an existing Search Folder

1. Right-click the folder, and then click **Customize This Search Folder**.
2. Modify the Search Folder name or criteria, and then click **OK**.

To update a Search Folder

→ In the **Folder List**, click the folder name.

Objective 1.3 practice tasks

There are no practice files for these tasks.

➤ Display your Outlook Inbox and do the following:

- ❑ Use the Instant Search feature to locate all messages in your Inbox that contain a specific term, such as <u>business</u>. Note that Outlook filters the messages as you enter the term and highlights the results in messages and message attachments.
- ❑ Expand the search to include all Outlook items.
- ❑ Refine the search to include only items dated this month.
- ❑ Refine the search to include only items that have attachments.

➤ Clear the search parameters and then do the following:

- ❑ Expand the *Search Folders* node and review the automatically created Search Folders.
- ❑ Create a Search Folder that displays all messages with attachments.
- ❑ Create a Search Folder that displays messages that were sent only to you and are marked as high importance.

Objective group 2
Manage messages

The skills tested in this section of the Microsoft Office Specialist exam for Microsoft Outlook 2016 relate to managing messages. Specifically, the following objectives are associated with this set of skills:

2.1 Configure mail settings

2.2 Create messages

2.3 Format messages

2.4 Organize and manage messages

The primary reason most people use Outlook is to send and receive email messages. Many people use email to keep in touch with friends and family, either from work or from home, and email has swiftly become an accepted and even required form of business communication. Outlook provides all the tools you need to send, respond to, organize, filter, sort, and otherwise manage messages.

Messages composed in Outlook 2016 can contain text, diagrams, and graphics and can be visually enhanced by colors, fonts, and backgrounds. You can configure Outlook to automatically include information such as your name, contact information, and company logo at the end of outgoing messages.

Outlook is designed to act as a complete information-management system; it provides many simple yet useful features that you can use to organize messages and other Outlook items and to quickly find information you need. Outlook automatically handles certain types of organization for you. You can organize items in Outlook by storing related items in folders and by assigning color categories to related items of all types. Outlook makes it easy to follow related messages from multiple people by displaying the messages in Conversation view.

This chapter guides you in studying ways of configuring your Outlook mail settings, automating processes to maximize email efficiency, and creating, customizing, formatting, organizing, and managing messages.

> To complete the practice tasks in this chapter, you need the practice files contained in the **MOSOutlook2016\Objective2** practice file folder. For more information, see "Download the practice files" in this book's introduction.

Objective 2.1: Configure mail settings

Set default fonts for outgoing messages

The fonts, styles, colors, and backgrounds of content you create in Outlook are governed by the Office theme. The default body font is 11-point Calibri. Outlook uses the default body font when composing messages. The default settings use a black font for new messages and a blue font for message responses (replies and forwards).

You can apply local character and paragraph formatting to message content. If you want to change the default appearance of text, you can specify the font, size, style, and color of the text of new messages and response messages (forwards and replies). You can continue to use different colors to visually differentiate between original message content and your responses within a message trail if you want to, or you might prefer to keep things clean and simple, and always use the same font regardless of whether a message is new; this simpler approach can help recipients to recognize message content from you.

You select message fonts and control other aspects of message responses on the Personal Stationery tab of the Signatures And Stationery dialog box.

Default fonts for outgoing messages

Exam Strategy Exam 77-731, "Outlook 2016: Core Communication, Collaboration and Email Skills," does not require you to demonstrate that you can set the default appearance of plain text message content.

To change the default font for outgoing messages

1. Open the **Outlook Options** dialog box and display the **Mail** page.

2. In the **Compose messages** section, click **Stationery and Fonts** to display the Personal Stationery tab of the Signatures And Stationery dialog box.

3. Do either of the following:

   - To set the font for new messages, click **Font** in the **New mail messages** section.

   - To set the font for message responses, click **Font** in the **Replying or forwarding messages** section.

4. In the **Font** dialog box, configure the font that you want Outlook to use for the selected message type. Then click **OK** in each of the open dialog boxes.

Create and assign automatic signatures

When you send an email message to someone, you will most likely "sign" the message by entering your name at the end of the message text. You can automatically insert your signature text in outgoing messages by creating an email signature and assigning it to your email account. Your email signature can include additional information (text and graphics) that you want to consistently provide to message recipients.

You can create multiple email signatures

You can have a different email signature for new messages and responses. If you have more than one email account set up in Outlook, you can instruct Outlook to insert a different signature in messages sent from each account.

See Also For information about manually inserting email signatures in messages, see "Objective 2.3: Format messages."

To create and assign automatic signatures

1. Open the **Outlook Options** dialog box and display the **Mail** page.
2. In the **Compose messages** section, click **Signatures**.
3. On the **Email Signature** tab of the **Signatures and Stationery** dialog box, click **New**.

> **Tip** Outlook user interface elements refer to electronic mail as *email* or *e-mail*. For consistency, the text of this book always references electronic mail as *email*.

4. In the **Type a name for this signature** box of the **New Signature** dialog box, enter a name that identifies the content or purpose of the signature, and then click **OK**.
5. In the **Edit signature** box, enter the signature text.
6. Format the signature text by selecting the text and then using the formatting commands at the top of the **Edit signature** area.

> **Tip** In email messages, your email signature will look exactly as it does in the Edit Signature pane.

7. If you want to include your electronic business card as part of your signature, click **Business Card**. Then in the **Insert Business Card** dialog box, locate and click your name, and click **OK**.
8. In the **Choose default signature** area, select the email account to which you want to assign the signature. Then in the **New messages** list, click the signature name.
9. If you want to include the signature in message responses, in the **Replies/forwards** list, click the signature name.
10. Make any other changes you want, and then click **OK** in each of the open dialog boxes.

To edit an automatic signature

1. Open the **Signatures and Stationery** dialog box and display the **Email Signature** tab.
2. In the **Select signatures to edit** box, click the signature you want to modify.
3. In the **Edit signature** box, modify the signature content and formatting.
4. In the **Choose default signature** section, modify the signature assignments.
5. Click **OK** in each of the open dialog boxes.

Automatically process and reply to messages

You can have Outlook evaluate your incoming or outgoing email messages and take various actions with them based on sets of instructions you set up, called *rules*. You can create rules based on different message criteria, such as the message sender, message recipients, message content, attachments, and importance. By using rules, you can have Outlook move, copy, delete, forward, redirect, reply to, or otherwise process messages based on the criteria you specify. You can choose from a collection of standard rules or create your own from scratch.

For any type of account, you can set up rules that manage the messages stored on your computer. For an Exchange Server account, you can set up rules that manage messages as your Exchange server receives or processes them, and rules that go into effect only when you indicate that you are unavailable, by setting up an Automatic Reply.

Configure rules for incoming and outgoing messages

You can create a rule based on one of the templates provided by Outlook, start from a blank rule, or copy and modify an existing rule.

Rules can process messages as you send them or as you receive them

41

To create a rule from scratch

1. On the **Info** page of the Backstage view, click **Manage Rules & Alerts**.

2. On the **Email Rules** page of the **Rules and Alerts** dialog box, click **New Rule**.

3. In the **Rules Wizard**, do one of the following, and then click **Next**:

   - In the **Stay Organized** or **Stay Up to Date** section of the **Select a template** list, click the template from which you want to build the new rule.

   - In the **Start from a blank rule** section of the **Select a template** list, click the type of message you want the rule to process.

4. In the **Select condition(s)** list, select the check box for each of the conditions that will identify messages to be processed by the rule. In the **Edit the rule description** area, click each underlined word or phrase, and replace it with a criterion that identifies the target messages. Then click **Next**.

5. In the **Select action(s)** list, select the check box for each of the actions you want Outlook to perform. Specify the criteria for the underlined words or phrases. Then click **Next**.

6. In the **Select exception(s)** list, select the check box for any condition that will identify messages to exclude from the rule action. Specify the criteria for the underlined words or phrases. Then click **Next**.

7. Specify a name for the new rule, do either of the following, and then click **Finish**:

   - Select the **Run this rule now on messages already in "Inbox"** check box.

   - Select the **Turn on this rule** check box.

To modify an existing rule

1. Open the **Rules and Alerts** dialog box. On the **Email Rules** page, in the **Rule** list, click the name of the rule you want to modify (do not select its check box). Click **Change Rule**, and then click **Edit Rule Settings**.

2. In the **Rules Wizard**, modify the rule as necessary.

To create a new rule based on an existing rule

1. Open the **Rules and Alerts** dialog box. On the **Email Rules** page, in the **Rule** list, click the name of the rule you want to use as the basis for the new rule. Then click **Copy**.

2. In the **Copy rule to** dialog box, if the **Folder** list includes multiple accounts or sets of accounts, click the account or set of accounts to which you want the rule to apply. Then click **OK**.

3. On the **Email Rules** page, with the copy selected, click **Change Rule**, and then click **Edit Rule Settings**.

4. In the **Rules Wizard**, modify the rule as necessary, and specify a unique name for the rule on the final page of the wizard.

To apply a rule to a specific account or set of accounts

1. In the **Rules and Alerts** dialog box, click the name of the rule for which you want to specify an account or set of accounts.

2. In the **Apply changes to this folder** list, click the account or set of accounts to which you want to apply the rule.

Tip The Apply Changes To This Folder list is present only when Outlook is configured to connect to multiple Exchange accounts.

To run a rule on existing messages

1. Open the **Rules and Alerts** dialog box. On the **Email Rules** page, click **Run Rules Now**.

2. In the **Run Rules Now** dialog box, select the check box of each rule you want to run, select the folder or folders and type of messages on which you want to run the rule or rules, and then click **Run Now**.

To delete a rule

1. Open the **Rules and Alerts** dialog box. On the **Email Rules** page, in the **Rule** list, click the name of the rule you want to delete, and then click **Delete**.

2. In the **Microsoft Outlook** dialog box that appears, click **Yes**.

Configure automatic replies and automatic reply rules

If your organization is running Microsoft Exchange Server, you can use the Automatic Replies feature to inform people who send you email messages of your availability. When you turn on the Automatic Replies feature, Outlook replies automatically to messages received from other people (but only to the first message from each person). You provide whatever textual information you want within the body of the automatic reply message (commonly referred to as an *out of office message*, or *OOF message*).

Configure Outlook to send separate automatic replies within and outside of your organization

---

Tip You can configure rules to send automatic responses from accounts other than Exchange Server accounts. For more information, see "Automatically process and reply to messages" earlier in this topic.

The functionality of the Automatic Replies feature is provided by Exchange Server, so the specific automatic reply options differ depending on what version of Exchange Server your organization is running. Regardless of which Exchange Server environment you're working in, this is a very useful feature. Your automatic reply message might also be displayed to co-workers in a MailTip at the top of messages they address to you, and displayed as part of your contact information in Microsoft Skype for Business.

The purpose of the Automatic Replies feature is to provide standard information to message senders. When you're away from your computer, an automatic reply can set expectations for when a correspondent can expect a personal response from you. You don't have to be physically out of the office to use this feature; some people use it to let other people know when responses will be delayed for other reasons, such as when they are working on a project that will prevent them from responding promptly to messages, or to inform customers who might be in different time zones of their standard working hours.

In addition to having Outlook send automatic replies, you can have it process messages that arrive while you are out of the office by using rules that are in effect only when the Automatic Replies feature is on.

The Automatic Replies feature is off until you explicitly turn it on; it does not coordinate with your free/busy information in the Calendar module.

When you are using an Exchange account, you can do the following when configuring Automatic Replies:

- You can create two auto-reply messages—one that Outlook sends only to people in your organization (on the same domain) and another sent either to everyone else or only to the people in your primary address book.

  When you have separate internal and external messages, you can distinguish the information made available to co-workers, to friends and business contacts, and to the general public (including senders of spam). For example, you might include your itinerary and mobile phone number only in an internal automatic reply, include your return date in a reply to your contacts, and not send any reply to other people.

- You can specify the font, size, and color of automatic reply message text and apply bold, italic, or underline formatting.

- You can format paragraphs as bulleted or numbered lists and control the indent level.

- You can specify start and end dates and times for your automatic reply message so that you don't have to remember to turn off Automatic Replies.

2

Separately from the Outlook rules that you run manually or automatically, you can set up rules that run only when the Automatic Replies feature is active. The Automatic Reply rules are built on a different set of criteria than standard Outlook rules; you can choose from a limited number of conditions, and you can't specify exceptions.

Create special rules to process and respond to messages when you're out of the office

To turn on automatic replies

1. On the **Info** page of the Backstage view, click **Automatic Replies**.

2. In the **Automatic Replies** dialog box, on the **Inside My Organization** page, click the **Send automatic replies** option.

3. Select the **Only send during this time range** check box.

4. Set the **Start time** to the date and time when you want to start sending automatic replies, and the **End time** to the date and time you want to stop.

5. In the content pane, enter and format the message you want to send to internal recipients.

6. On the **Outside My Organization** page, select the **Auto-reply to people outside my organization** check box.

7. If you want to restrict automatic replies to only email messages that are in your Contacts address book, click the **My Contacts only** option.

8. In the content pane, enter and format the message you want to send to external recipients.

9. In the **Automatic Replies** dialog box, click **OK**.

To create a rule that runs only when you are out of the office

1. On the **Info** page of the Backstage view, click **Automatic Replies**.

2. In the **Automatic Replies** dialog box, click **Rules**.

3. In the **Automatic Reply Rules** dialog box, click **Add Rule**.

4. In the **When a message arrives that meets the following conditions** area of the **Edit Rule** dialog box, specify the conditions that define messages to be processed by the rule.

5. To specify additional conditions such as message size, receipt date, importance, and sensitivity, click **Advanced** and, in the **Advanced** dialog box, specify the conditions, and then click **OK**.

6. In the **Perform these actions** area of the **Edit Rule** dialog box, specify the actions to be performed by the rule.

7. Click **OK** in each of the three open dialog boxes (**Edit Rule**, **Automatic Reply Rules**, and **Automatic Replies**).

To specify rules to run while Automatic Replies are turned on

1. On the **Info** page of the Backstage view, click **Automatic Replies**.

2. In the **Automatic Replies** dialog box, click **Rules**.

3. In the **Automatic Reply Rules** dialog box, select the check box for each rule you want to run, and clear the check box for each rule you don't want to run during the current out-of-office period. Then click **OK** in the **Automatic Reply Rules** and **Automatic Replies** dialog boxes.

Populate messages by using Quick Parts

You can save information and document elements that you use frequently as custom building blocks so that you can easily insert them into documents. A custom building block can be a simple phrase or sentence that you use often, or it can include full paragraphs of text and objects such as graphics. You need to create the element exactly as you want it only one time; then you can save it as a building block and use it confidently wherever you need it.

You insert a custom building block into a message from the Quick Parts gallery on the Quick Parts menu.

To create a building block, you create and select the item you want to save, click Save Selection To Quick Parts Gallery on the Quick Parts menu, and assign a name to the building block. You can then insert the building block at the cursor by entering the building block name and pressing F3, or by displaying the Quick Parts gallery and clicking the thumbnail of the building block you want. Or you can insert it elsewhere by right-clicking the thumbnail in the gallery and then clicking one of the specified locations.

To create Quick Parts

1. In a message composition window, enter and format the content you want to save as a Quick Part.

2. Select the content.

3. On the **Insert** tab, in the **Text** group, click the **Quick Parts** button, and then click **Save Selection to Quick Part Gallery**.

4. In the **Create New Building Block** dialog box, do the following, and then click **OK**:

    a. In the **Name** box, enter a name for the building block.

    b. In the **Description** box, enter a description that will appear as a ScreenTip when you point to the building block in the Quick Parts gallery.

Modify Building Block	? ✕
Name:	Driving Directions
Gallery:	Quick Parts ⌄
Category:	General ⌄
Description:	Link to map and driving directions
Save in:	NormalEmail ⌄
Options:	Insert content only ⌄
	OK Cancel

Save frequently used message content as Quick Parts that you can insert in any message

To insert Quick Parts

→ Enter the building block name, and then press **F3**.

→ On the **Insert** tab, in the **Text** group, click the **Quick Parts** button, and then click the building block you want to insert.

Manage junk email

By default, when Outlook receives a message that it deems to be either junk mail or a phishing message, it delivers that message to the Junk Email folder associated with your account rather than to your Inbox. (Each account you configure Outlook to connect to has its own Junk Email folder.) When the Junk Email folder contains one or more messages, the number of messages in the folder is shown in parentheses at the end of the folder name. If any of the messages in the folder have not been read, the folder name is bold.

Outlook converts message content in the Junk Email folder to plain text and disables any active links or content within the message. The InfoBar in the message header provides specific information about the message's status.

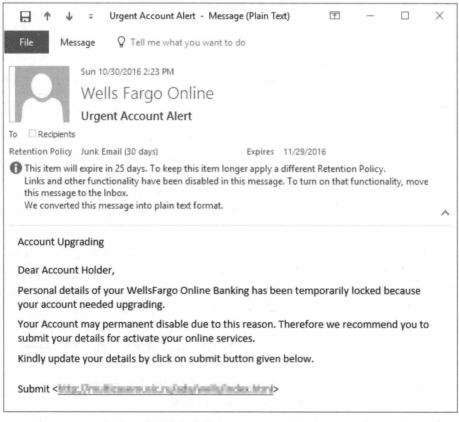

Outlook removes attachments, disables links, and exposes target URLs for your review

Any remote graphics (graphics that are displayed from Internet locations rather than embedded in the message—sometimes called *web beacons*) that were present in the message are converted to URLs, which reveals where the graphics originated.

Although the response options on the ribbon are active, you can't reply to a message from the Junk Email folder—you must first move it to the Inbox or another folder. You can delete messages from the Junk Email folder, or forward a message from the folder to someone else who can verify for you whether the message is valid. The forwarded message will be in plain-text format rather than in the original message format.

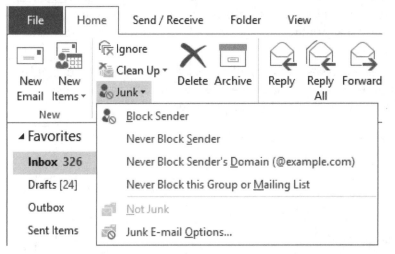

From the Junk menu, you can block or allow specific senders or sending domains

You manage junk mail settings from the Junk Email Options dialog box. You set specific junk email processing options for each email account to which Outlook is configured to connect. The account for which you're configuring options is shown in the title bar of the Junk Email Options dialog box. The Junk Email Options dialog box has five tabs:

- **Options** On this tab, you set the junk mail filtering level and specify the actions Outlook should take with messages that the junk mail filter retains.
- **Safe Senders** On this tab, you specify sending email addresses or domains from which Outlook should never filter messages.
- **Safe Recipients** On this tab, you specify recipient email addresses at which you might receive messages, such as a distribution lists, that Outlook should never filter.
- **Blocked Senders** On this tab, you specify sending email addresses or domains from which Outlook should always block messages.
- **International** On this tab, you specify country-specific or region-specific top-level domains from which Outlook should always block messages, or incoming message languages, that you want Outlook to always block.

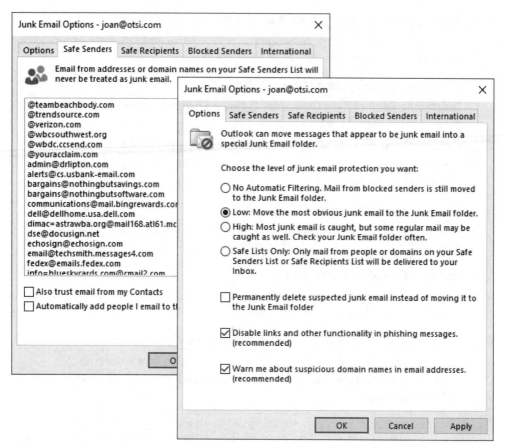

Tailor the junk mail filter settings to fit your typical email patterns

To process a junk email message

1. In the **Junk Email** folder, select the message you want to process.
2. On the **Home** tab, in the **Delete** group, click the **Junk** button.
3. In the **Junk** list, click one of the following:

   - **Block Sender** to add the message sender to the Blocked Senders list.
   - **Never Block Sender** to add the message sender to the Safe Senders list.
   - **Never Block Sender's Domain** to add the message sender's domain to the Safe Senders list.
   - **Never Block this Group or Mailing List** to add the recipient group to the Safe Recipients list.
   - **Not Junk** to move the message to the Inbox. You then have the option of adding the message sender to the Safe Senders list.

To configure junk mail settings for the sender of an open message

→ On the **Message** tab of the message reading window, in the **Delete** group, click the **Junk** button, and then click the option you want.

To empty the Junk Email folder of any mailbox

1. Display the **Folder List** in the **Folder Pane** and expand the mailbox to display its Junk Email folder.

2. Right-click the **Junk Email** folder, and then click **Empty Folder**.

3. In the message box that appears, click **Yes** to confirm that you want to permanently delete the items.

To open the Junk Email Options dialog box

→ On the **Home** tab, in the **Delete** group, on the **Junk** menu, click **Junk Email Options**.

To choose a junk email protection level

→ On the **Options** tab of the **Junk Email Options** dialog box, click **No Automatic Filtering**, **Low**, **High**, or **Safe Lists Only**.

To configure Outlook to automatically delete suspected junk email

→ On the **Options** tab of the **Junk Email Options** dialog box, select the **Permanently delete suspected junk email instead of moving it to the Junk Email folder** check box.

Tip Do not select the Permanently Delete Suspected Junk Email... check box if you set the protection level to High or to Safe Lists Only. With these settings, it is likely that the Junk Email Filter will catch quite a few valid messages that you don't want deleted.

To ensure that messages from a specific sender or domain aren't classified as junk

1. On the **Safe Senders** tab of the **Junk Email Options** dialog box, click **Add**.

2. In the **Add address or domain** dialog box, enter an email address (for example, *tom@contoso.com*) or domain (for example, *@contoso.com*), and then click **OK**.

To ensure that responses to messages you send aren't classified as junk

→ On the **Safe Senders** tab of the **Junk Email Options** dialog box, select the **Automatically add people I email to the Safe Senders List** check box.

To ensure that messages sent to a specific email address or domain aren't filtered

1. On the **Safe Recipients** tab of the **Junk Email Options** dialog box, click **Add**.

2. In the **Add address or domain** dialog box, enter an email address or domain, and then click **OK**.

Tip Add distribution lists or mailing lists of which you are a member to your Safe Recipients List to ensure that messages sent to you through the distribution list or mailing list will never be treated as junk email.

To ensure that messages from a specific sender or domain are always classified as junk

1. On the **Blocked Senders** tab of the **Junk Email Options** dialog box, click **Add**.

2. In the **Add address or domain** dialog box, enter an email address or domain, and then click **OK**.

To block all messages from a location-specific top-level domain

1. On the **International** tab of the **Junk Email Options** dialog box, click **Blocked Top-Level Domain List**.

2. In the **Blocked Top-Level Domain List** dialog box, select the check box for the top-level domain of each country or region you want to block, and then click **OK**.

To block all messages with language-specific encoding

1. On the **International** tab of the **Junk Email Options** dialog box, click **Blocked Encodings List**.

2. In the **Blocked Encodings List** dialog box, select the check box for each language you want to block, and then click **OK**.

2

Objective 2.1 practice tasks

There are no practice files for these tasks. Before you begin, alert a colleague that you're going to practice creating automatic replies and rules.

➤ Start Outlook and do the following:

❑ Set the default font for new messages to Green, 12-point Candara.

❑ Create an email signature that includes your standard email message closure (such as *Best regards* or *Thanks!*) and your name. Assign the email signature to new messages sent from your primary account.

❑ Configure Outlook to automatically reply to messages sent to your primary account for the next hour. For messages received from senders inside your organization, enter the automatic reply text <u>Thank you for your message. I'm studying for the Outlook MOS certification exam and will check messages soon.</u> Turn off automatic replies to senders outside of your organization.

❑ Create a rule that assigns all incoming messages from your colleague to the Red category, or to another category of your choosing. Turn on the rule.

➤ Create a new email message to your colleague and do the following:

❑ Verify that the message includes the email signature you configured earlier.

❑ In the message content pane, above the email signature, enter <u>Please help me test Outlook automatic replies and rules by responding to this message.</u>

❑ Verify that the message text uses the default font you configured earlier.

❑ Before sending the message, save the message content (including the text and your email signature) as a Quick Part named <u>Test Message</u>.

❑ Delete the message content and then reinsert it by using the Quick Part.

❑ Send the message.

➤ When your colleague responds to the message, do the following:

❑ Verify that Outlook assigns the response message to the category you selected earlier.

❑ From the response message, add your colleague's email address to your Safe Senders list.

➤ Display your Junk Email folder and do the following:

❑ Locate a message from a sender you want to block.

❑ Add the message sender to your Blocked Senders list.

❑ If your Junk Email folder contains no messages you want to keep, empty it.

Objective 2.2: Create messages

Create and send messages

You can send a message from any account for which you have permission. Valid sending accounts include those that are configured on your computer and other accounts for which you have been delegated permission.

> **See Also**   For information about sending from alternative accounts, see "Manage multiple accounts" in "Objective 1.1: Customize settings." For information about delegating permission to accounts, see "Delegate access" in "Objective 2.4: Organize and manage messages."

In addition to the To and Cc fields, which are displayed by default in the message composition window, you can display the From field and the Bcc field. When you display or hide these optional message header fields in an individual message, Outlook retains the setting for all message composition windows.

A message with all available header fields and an automatic signature

A convenient way to distribute a file (such as a Microsoft Word document, Excel workbook, PowerPoint presentation, or picture) is by attaching the file to an email message. Message recipients can preview or open the file from the Reading Pane, open it from the message window, forward it to other people, or save it to their computers.

When you attach a file from a shared online location, such as a OneDrive folder or SharePoint document library, the message may be attached as a link to the shared file, indicated by a cloud on the file icon. If you prefer to send the file, you can convert the link to a freestanding attachment.

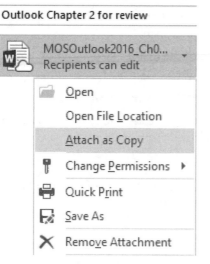

Converting a shared file to an attachment

You can also attach Outlook items, such as other messages, calendar items, contact records, notes, and tasks, to outgoing messages. Recipients can save attached items in their own Outlook installations.

To create an original message

→ In the Mail module, on the **Home** tab, in the **New** group, click **New Email**.

→ In the Mail module, press **Ctrl+N**.

→ In any module, on the **Home** tab, in the **New** group, click **New Items**, and then click **Email Message**.

> **Tip** Outlook user interface elements refer to electronic mail as *email* or *e-mail*. For consistency, the text of this book always references electronic mail as *email*.

→ In any module, press **Ctrl+Shift+M**.

To display optional address fields

→ On the **Options** tab of the message window, in the **Show Fields** group, click **Bcc**.

To attach one or more files to a message

→ Drag the file or files you want to attach to the message from File Explorer into the message area of the message window.

Or

1. On the **Message** tab or **Insert** tab of the message window, in the **Include** group, click **Attach File**.

2. On the **Attach File** menu, do one of the following:

   - If the file you want to attach is in the **Recent Items** list, click the file in the list.

   - Click **Browse Web Locations**, click the file storage location, and browse to and select the file you want to attach.

   - Click **Browse This PC** to open the **Insert File** dialog box. Locate and click the file you want to attach, and then click **Insert**.

To attach a separate copy of a shared file to a message

→ In the **Attached** area of the message header, point to the attachment, click the arrow that appears, and then click **Attach as Copy**.

To attach an Outlook item to a message

→ Drag the item you want to attach to the message from the content pane into the message area of the message window.

Or

1. Do either of the following:

   - On the **Message** tab of the message window, in the **Include** group, click **Attach Item**, and then click **Outlook Item**.

   - On the **Insert** tab of the message window, in the **Include** group, click **Outlook Item**.

2. In the **Insert Item** dialog box, locate and click the item you want to attach.

3. With **Attachment** selected in the **Insert as** area, click **OK**.

To remove an attachment from an outgoing email message

→ In the **Attached** area of the message header, point to the file attachment, click the arrow that appears, and then click **Remove Attachment**.

To recall a message

1. From your **Sent Items** folder, open the message you want to recall.

2. On the **Message** tab, in the **Move** group, click the **More Move Actions** button, and then click **Recall This Message**.

> **Recall This Message** ✕
>
> **Some recipients may have already read this message.**
>
> ---
>
> Message recall can delete or replace copies of this message in recipient Inboxes, if they have not yet read this message.
>
> Are you sure you want to
>
> ⦿ Delete unread copies of this message
>
> ○ Delete unread copies and replace with a new message
>
> ☑ Tell me if recall succeeds or fails for each recipient
>
> OK   Cancel

You can delete or replace a message you've sent if it hasn't yet been read by the recipient

3. In the **Recall This Message** dialog box, select an option to indicate whether you want to delete or replace the sent message, and whether you want to receive an email notification of the success or failure of each recall. Then click **OK**.

4. If you choose to replace the message, a new message window opens. Enter the content that you want to include in the replacement message, and then send it.

Configure message options

When you send a message, you can include visual indicators of the importance, sensitivity, or subject category of a message or other Outlook item, flag a message for follow-up, restrict other people from changing or forwarding message content, provide a simple feedback mechanism in the form of voting buttons, and specify message delivery options to fit your needs.

Common message settings and delivery options include the following:

- **Flags and reminders** You can place an outgoing message on your task list, add an informational reminder to it, or set a reminder to appear at a certain time and date, for yourself and for message recipients.

- **Importance** You can indicate the urgency of a message by setting its importance to High or Low. A corresponding banner appears in the message header and, if the Importance field is included in the view, an importance icon appears in the Inbox or other message folder.

- **Sensitivity** You can indicate that a message should be kept private by setting its sensitivity to Confidential, Personal, or Private. No indicator appears in the message folder, but a banner appears in the message header to indicate a sensitivity level other than Normal.

- **Security** If you have a digital ID, you can digitally sign the message; or you can encrypt the contents of the message.

- **Voting options** If you and your message recipients have Microsoft Exchange Server accounts, you can add voting buttons to your messages so that recipients can quickly select from multiple-choice response options.

- **Tracking options** You can track messages by requesting delivery receipts and read receipts. These receipts are messages automatically generated by the recipient's email server when it delivers the message to the recipient and when the recipient opens the message.

- **Delivery options** You can have reply messages delivered to an email address other than yours, specify a date and time for the message to be delivered and to expire, and set advanced attachment format and encoding options.

- **Categories** You can assign a message to a color category that will be visible to the recipient if he or she views the message in Outlook.

Exam Strategy Exam 77-731, "Outlook 2016: Core Communication, Collaboration and Email Skills," does not require you to demonstrate the ability to schedule the delivery of a message or set an expiration time for a message.

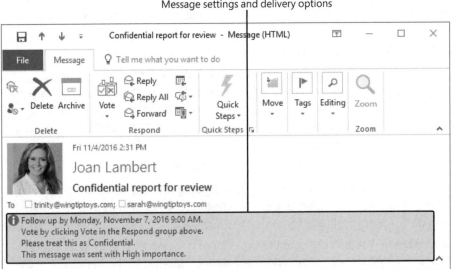

Message settings and delivery options

The message header provides important information to recipients

The most commonly used options are available in the Tags group on the Message tab of the message window. You can access other options from the Properties dialog box, which you open by clicking the Tags dialog box launcher.

Settings in the Properties dialog box are specific to the current message

To designate a message as high or low priority

→ On the **Message** tab of the message window, in the **Tags** group, click the **High Importance** or **Low Importance** button.

Or

1. On the **Message** tab of the message window, click the **Tags** dialog box launcher.

2. In the **Properties** dialog box, click the option you want in the **Importance** list, and then click **Close**.

To remove the priority setting from a message you are forwarding

1. On the **Message** tab of the received message window, in the **Respond** group, click the **Forward** button.

2. On the **Message** tab of the forwarded message composition window, in the **Tags** group, click the active **High Importance** or **Low Importance** button to turn it off.

To set the sensitivity of a message

1. On the **Message** tab of the message window, click the **Tags** dialog box launcher.

2. In the **Properties** dialog box, click the option you want in the **Sensitivity** list, and then click **Close**.

Tip You can set the default sensitivity and priority of all new messages in the Send Messages section of the Mail page of the Outlook Options dialog box.

To flag an outgoing message for follow-up by you

➔ On the **Message** tab of the message window, click the **Follow Up** button, and then click the flag date you want to set.

To flag an outgoing message for follow-up by recipients

1. On the **Message** tab of the message window, click the **Follow Up** button, and then click **Custom**.

2. In the **Custom** dialog box, select the **Flag for Recipients** check box.

3. If you want to set a reminder for recipients, select the **Reminder** check box and the reminder date and time.

4. Click **OK** to set the flag, which will appear in the message header as *Recipients receive: Follow up* or *Recipients receive: Follow up by* followed by the specified date and time.

To add voting options to a message

➔ On the **Options** tab of the message window, in the **Tracking** group, click **Use Voting Buttons**, and then click the existing combination of voting buttons you want.

Or

1. Do either of the following:

    • On the **Options** tab, click the **More Options** dialog box launcher.

    • On the **Options** tab of the message window, in the **Tracking** group, click **Use Voting Buttons**, and then click **Custom**.

2. In the **Voting and Tracking options** area of the **Properties** dialog box, select the **Use voting buttons** check box.

3. In the **Use voting buttons** list, do either of the following:

    • Click the combination of voting buttons you want in the list.

    • Enter the voting button labels you want, separated by semicolons.

4. Close the **Properties** dialog box.

To request a message receipt

1. On the **Options** tab, click the **More Options** dialog box launcher.

2. In the **Voting and Tracking options** area of the **Properties** dialog box, do either of the following:

    • Select the **Request a delivery receipt for this message** check box to request notification when the message is delivered to the recipient's mailbox.

    • Select the **Request a read receipt for this message** check box to request notification when the message is marked as read.

3. Close the **Properties** dialog box.

To direct responses to an alternative email address

1. Do either of the following:
   - On the **Options** tab, in the **More Options** group, click **Direct Replies To**.
   - On the **Options** tab, click the **More Options** dialog box launcher.
2. In the **Delivery options** area of the **Properties** dialog box, enter the email address to which you want responses to be delivered in the **Have replies sent to** box.
3. Close the **Properties** dialog box.

Respond to messages

After you read a message, Outlook indicates its status as Read by removing the bold formatting and blue bar from the message header. You can change the read status of a message to provide visual cues or to affect the number that appears after the folder name in the Folder Pane.

You can respond to most email messages that you receive by clicking a response button either in the Reading Pane, in the Respond group on the Home tab of the program window, or in the Respond group on the Message tab of the message window.

The most standard response to a message is a reply. When you reply to a message, Outlook fills in one or more of the address boxes for you, as follows:

- **Reply** Creates an email message, addressed to only the original message sender, that contains the original message text.

- **Reply All** Creates an email message, addressed to the message sender and all recipients listed in the To and Cc boxes, that contains the original message text. The message is not addressed to recipients of blind courtesy copies (Bcc recipients).

- **Reply with Meeting** Creates a meeting invitation addressed to all message recipients. The message text is included in the meeting window content pane. Outlook suggests the current date and an upcoming half-hour time slot for the meeting.

Message replies include the original message header and text, preceded by a space in which you can respond. Replies do not include any attachments from the original message.

You can add, change, and delete recipients from any reply before sending it.

You can forward a received message to any email address (regardless of whether the recipient uses Outlook) provided the message was not sent with restricted permissions.

2

Outlook 2016 has the following message-forwarding options:

- **Forward** Creates a new message that contains the text of the original, and retains any attachments from the original message.

- **Forward As Attachment** Creates a blank message that contains no text but includes the original message as an attachment. The original message text and any attachments are available to the new recipient when he or she opens the attached message.

When you forward a message, Outlook does not fill in the recipient boxes for you (the assumption being that you want to forward the message to someone who wasn't included on the original message).

To mark messages as read or unread

1. Select the message or messages for which you want to change the status.
2. Right-click the selection, and then click **Mark as Read** or **Mark as Unread**.

To reply only to the message sender

→ On the **Home** tab, in the **Respond** group, click the **Reply** button.

→ In the **Reading Pane**, in the message header, click the **Reply** button.

→ Press **Ctrl+R**.

To reply to all message recipients

→ On the **Home** tab, in the **Respond** group, click the **Reply All** button.

→ In the **Reading Pane**, in the message header, click the **Reply All** button.

→ Press **Ctrl+Shift+R**.

To forward a message

→ On the **Home** tab, in the **Respond** group, click the **Forward** button.

→ In the **Reading Pane**, in the message header, click the **Forward** button.

→ Press **Ctrl+F**.

To delete messages

1. Select the message, messages, or conversation you want to delete.
2. Do either of the following:
   - Press the **Delete** key.
   - On the **Home** tab, in the **Delete** group, click **Delete**.
3. If prompted to confirm the deletion, click **Yes**.

Objective 2.2 practice tasks

The practice files for these tasks are located in the **MOSOutlook2016\Objective2** practice file folder. Before you begin, alert a colleague that you will be practicing sending messages.

➤ Start Outlook and do the following:

❑ Create a new message with the subject <u>MOS Sensitivity</u> and address the message to yourself.

❑ Flag the message as personal.

❑ Configure the message to expire in five minutes, and then send it.

➤ After you receive the MOS Sensitivity message, do the following:

❑ Open and then close the message.

❑ Wait for the message to expire, and note the effect of the expiration.

❑ Mark the message as unread.

➤ Create a new message to yourself with the subject <u>MOS Secret</u>, and do the following:

❑ Flag the message as both high priority and confidential.

❑ Send the message.

➤ After you receive the MOS Secret message, do the following:

❑ Forward the message.

❑ Address the forwarded message to your colleague.

❑ Change the priority to Normal.

❑ Add yourself as a BCC recipient.

❑ Request a delivery receipt.

❑ Send the message.

➤ After the message arrives, do the following:

❑ Open the message and verify that the message header doesn't include you as a message recipient.

❑ Verify that you receive delivery receipts for yourself and your colleague.

❑ Attempt to recall the message, and note the results.

➤ Create a new message to yourself with the subject <u>MOS Vote</u>, and do the following:

❏ In the message content pane, enter <u>Will I pass the Outlook MOS exam?</u>

❏ Configure the message options to include the custom voting buttons <u>I Will</u>, <u>I Might</u>, and <u>I Will Not</u>.

❏ Send the message.

❏ After you receive the message, respond by voting *I Will*.

❏ Locate and review the poll results.

➤ Create a new message to yourself with the subject <u>MOS Files</u>, and do the following:

❏ Attach the **Outlook_2-2a** document to the message.

❏ Use a different technique to attach the **Outlook_2-2b** presentation to the message.

❏ Send the message to yourself.

❏ After you receive the message, preview each of the attachments in the Reading Pane. Scroll through the full content of each.

❏ Open the **Outlook_2-2a** document and **Outlook_2-2b** presentation. Scroll through the document and run the slide show to identify any differences between the preview and the file content.

➤ Create a new message to yourself with the subject <u>MOS Items</u>, and do the following:

❏ Attach any contact record (not a business card) and any calendar item (not a calendar) to the message.

❏ Send the message.

❏ After you receive the message, preview each of the attachments in the Reading Pane.

❏ Open the contact record.

➤ Close the open document, presentation, contact record, and email messages.

Objective 2.3: Format messages

Format text

You can manually format text in the message content pane to differentiate it from your default font. The local formatting options available in Outlook 2016 are the same as those available in Word 2016, PowerPoint 2016, and other Office 2016 programs. You might already be familiar with the formatting options from working with those programs. Here's a quick review of the types of formatting changes you can make.

- **Font, size, and color** More than 220 fonts in a range of sizes and in a virtually unlimited selection of colors
- **Font style** Regular, bold, italic, or bold italic
- **Underline style and color** Plain, multiple, dotted, dashed, wavy, and many combinations thereof, in all colors
- **Effects** Strikethrough, superscript, subscript, shadow, outline, emboss, engrave, small caps, all caps, or hidden
- **Character spacing** Scale, spacing, position, and kerning
- **Paragraph attributes** Alignment, indentation, and spacing
- **Character and paragraph styles** Titles, headings, and purpose-specific font formatting (for example, for quotes and book titles)

To apply local formatting to selected text

→ On the **Mini Toolbar**, click or select the formatting you want to apply.

→ In the **Basic Text** group the **Message** tab, or in the **Font** or **Paragraph** group on the **Format Text** tab, click or select the formatting option.

→ On the **Message** tab, click the **Basic Text** dialog box launcher. On the **Font** and **Advanced** tabs of the **Font** dialog box, click or select the formatting you want to apply, and then click **OK**.

→ On the **Format Text** tab, click the **Font** dialog box launcher. In the **Font** dialog box, click or select the formatting you want to apply, and then click **OK**.

→ On the **Format Text** tab, click the **Paragraph** dialog box launcher. On the **Indents and Spacing** and **Line and Page Breaks** tabs of the **Paragraph** dialog box, click or select the formatting you want to apply, and then click **OK**.

2

To apply existing formatting to other text

1. In the message composition window, position the cursor in the formatted text or paragraph.

2. Do either of the following:

   - On the **Message** tab or **Format Text** tab, in the **Clipboard** group, click the **Format Painter** button to store the character and paragraph formatting of the selected text or active paragraph for a single use.

   - In the **Clipboard** group, double-click the **Format Painter** button to store the formatting of the selected text or active paragraph for multiple uses.

3. Drag the paintbrush-shaped cursor across the text to which you want to apply the stored formatting.

4. If necessary, click the **Format Painter** button or press the **Esc** key to turn off the Format Painter tool.

Tip When you are working with certain content elements such as tables and graphics, one or more tool tabs containing formatting commands specific to that element appear on the ribbon. You must select the element to access its formatting commands.

Apply themes

You can change the appearance of the text in a message by applying either local formatting (character or paragraph attributes and styles that you apply directly to text) or global formatting (a theme that you apply to the entire document) in the same way that you would when working in a Word document or PowerPoint presentation.

Nine of the standard Microsoft Office 2016 themes (which are not the same as the email message themes you can select in the Theme Or Stationery dialog box) are available from the Themes gallery on the Options tab in a message composition window. Each theme controls the colors, fonts, and graphic effects used in the message.

The default theme for all email messages, Word documents, PowerPoint presentations, Excel workbooks, and other Office 2016 documents is the Office theme. If you don't apply another theme to your message, the colors, fonts, and effects in your message are controlled by the Office theme.

To specify an email theme or stationery for HTML messages

1. Open the **Outlook Options** dialog box and display the **Mail** page.

2. In the **Compose messages** section, click **Stationery and Fonts**.

3. On the **Personal Stationery** tab of the **Signatures and Stationery** dialog box, in the **Theme or stationery for new HTML email message** area, click **Theme**.

Tip Outlook user interface elements refer to electronic mail as *email* or *e-mail*. For consistency, the text of this book always references electronic mail as *email*.

---

4. In the **Theme or Stationery** dialog box, click the theme you want to use. Select or clear the **Vivid Colors**, **Active Graphics**, and **Background Image** check boxes to specify the theme elements you want to include, and then click **OK**.

5. In the **Theme or stationery for new HTML email message** area, click the **Font** arrow, and then do one of the following:

   - Click **Use theme's font** to use the theme font for new messages and responses.

   - Click **Use my font when replying and forwarding messages** to use the theme font for new messages and a custom font for responses.

   - Click **Always use my font** to use a custom font for all messages and to use only the styles, colors, and backgrounds of the selected theme.

6. Click **OK** in the open dialog boxes.

To apply a theme to an individual message

→ In the message composition window, on the **Options** tab, in the **Themes** group, click the **Themes** button, and then click the theme you want to apply.

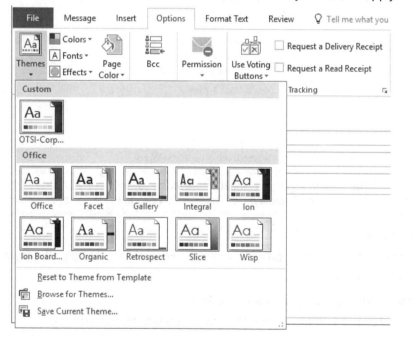

Apply a custom or built-in theme to any message

To reset to the default theme

1. On the **Personal Stationery** tab of the **Signatures and Stationery** dialog box, in the **Theme or stationery for new HTML email message** area, click **Theme**.

2. In the **Theme or Stationery** dialog box, click **(No Theme)**, and then click **OK**.

Apply styles

A style is a combination of character formatting and paragraph formatting that you can apply to selected text or the active paragraph with one click. You can use styles to format text in email messages in the same way that you do in Word documents.

Outlook supports the same styles and style sets that are available in Word

Exam Strategy If the existing styles don't meet your needs, you can modify existing styles and create styles from scratch. Modifying and creating styles is beyond the scope of this exam.

To display the Styles pane

→ In the message composition window, on the **Format Text** tab, click the **Styles** dialog box launcher.

To preview the effect of a style on selected text

→ On the **Format Text** tab, in the **Quick Styles** gallery, point to the style.

To apply a style to selected text

→ In the **Quick Styles** gallery or in the **Styles** pane, click the style.

Create hyperlinks

Outlook automatically converts URLs that you enter in a message content pane into hyperlinks that the recipient can click to display the webpage. You can manually create a hyperlink from any text or graphic to a heading or bookmark within the message or to an external file or webpage. You can also create a hyperlink that the recipient can click to create a new email message that already has the To and Subject fields populated.

To begin creating a hyperlink of any type

1. Select the text or graphic from which you want to link.

2. Do either of the following to open the Insert Hyperlink dialog box:

   - On the **Insert** tab, in the **Links** group, click **Hyperlink**.
   - Press **Ctrl+K**.

To create a hyperlink to an existing file

1. In the **Insert Hyperlink** dialog box, in the **Link to** list, click **Existing File or Web Page**.

2. Do either of the following:

   - In the **Look in** pane, browse to the file you want to link to.
   - Click the **Browse for File** button and then, in the **Link to File** dialog box, browse to the file and click **Open**.

3. In the **Insert Hyperlink** dialog box, click **OK**.

To create a Word document and a hyperlink to it

1. In the **Insert Hyperlink** dialog box, in the **Link to** list, click **Create New Document**.

2. In the **Name of new document** box, enter a name for the document.

3. To create the document in a folder other than your Documents folder, click **Change**, browse to the folder in which you want to save the file, and then click **OK**.

4. In the **When to edit** area, do one of the following:

   - Click **Edit the new document later** to create a blank document.
   - Click **Edit the new document now** to create a document and open it in Word.

5. In the **Insert Hyperlink** dialog box, click **OK**.

To create a hyperlink to a webpage

1. In the **Insert Hyperlink** dialog box, in the **Link to** list, click **Existing File or Web Page**.

2. Do either of the following:

   - In the **Address** box, enter the URL of the webpage you want to link to.
   - Click the **Browse the Web** button. In the web browser window that opens, display the webpage you want to link to. Then minimize or close the browser window.

3. In the **Insert Hyperlink** dialog box, click **OK**.

To create a hyperlink to a heading or bookmark within the message

1. In the **Insert Hyperlink** dialog box, in the **Link to** list, click **Place in This Document**.

2. In the **Select a place in this document** box, click the heading or bookmark you want to link to.

3. In the **Insert Hyperlink** dialog box, click **OK**.

To create a hyperlink that creates a pre-addressed email message

1. In the **Insert Hyperlink** dialog box, in the **Link to** list, click **Email Address**.

2. In the **Email address** box, enter the name or email address of the message recipient.

3. In the **Subject** box, enter the message subject.

4. In the **Insert Hyperlink** dialog box, click **OK**.

To change the target of an existing hyperlink

1. Right-click the hyperlinked text or graphic, and then click **Edit Hyperlink**.

2. In the **Edit Hyperlink** dialog box, change the properties of the hyperlink, and then click **OK**.

To remove a hyperlink

→ Right-click the hyperlinked text or graphic, and then click **Remove Hyperlink**.

Insert images

Email is a means of communicating information to other people, and, as the old saying goes, a picture is worth a thousand words. Using Outlook 2016, you can communicate visual information in the following ways:

- Share photographs with other people by attaching the photos to messages or embedding them in messages.

- Share information from websites, documents, and other visual presentations by capturing images of your screen directly from Outlook and then inserting those images in your message.

- Explain complicated processes and other business information by creating SmartArt graphics within messages or by embedding SmartArt graphics that you create in other Office 2016 programs.

- Communicate statistical information by creating a chart within a message.

- Decorate message content by inserting clip art images.

You can insert all these types of images from the Illustrations group on the Insert tab into the content pane of an email message, calendar item, or task, or into the notes pane of a contact record.

Exam Strategy Capturing screenshots, inserting SmartArt graphics or charts, and formatting images are beyond the scope of this exam.

You can insert digital photographs or pictures created in almost any program into an Outlook email message. You specify the source of the picture you want to insert by clicking one of the following two buttons, which are located in the Illustrations group on the Insert tab:

- **Pictures** Click this button to insert a picture that is saved as a file on your computer, on a network drive, or on a device (such as a digital camera) that is connected to your computer.

- **Online Pictures** Click this button to insert a royalty-free clip art image from Office.com, a web search result from Bing, or an image stored in your personal online storage folder or another online source.

After inserting a picture from a file or from an online source, you can modify the picture and control the flow of text around it by using the commands on the Format tool tab that appears when the picture is selected.

You can modify pictures in outgoing messages in the same ways that you can in Word documents

To insert an image from a file

1. Click in the message content pane.

2. On the **Insert** tab, in the **Illustrations** group, click **Pictures**.

3. In the **Insert Picture** dialog box, browse to and click the file you want. Then do one of the following:

   - To insert the image in the message content pane, click **Insert**.

   - To insert an image that updates automatically if the image file changes, in the **Insert** list, click **Link to File**.

   - To insert an image that you can manually update if the image file changes, in the **Insert** list, click **Insert and Link**.

To insert an online image

1. On the **Insert** tab, in the **Illustrations** group, click **Online Pictures**.

2. In the **Insert Pictures** window, click the online source.

3. Enter a keyword in the search box and press **Enter**, or browse to the picture you want to insert.

4. Double-click the image you want to insert.

> **Tip** You change the size, shape, and location of an image by using the same techniques as you do with other graphic elements.

Insert signatures

After you create a signature, you can manually add it to any email message. Inserting a signature in a message automatically replaces any signature that is already in the message.

> **See Also** For information about creating and assigning email signatures, see "Objective 2.1: Configure mail settings."

To manually insert an existing email signature in a message

1. Position the cursor where you want to insert the email signature.

2. On the **Insert** tab, in the **Include** group, click the **Signature** button.

3. In the **Signature** list, click the name of the email signature you want to insert.

To remove an email signature from a message

→ Select and delete the signature content as you would any other text.

Objective 2.3 practice tasks

The practice file for these tasks is located in the **MOSOutlook2016\Objective2** practice file folder.

➤ Start Outlook, create a new message to yourself with the subject <u>MOS Formatting</u>, and do the following:

❑ Open the **Outlook_2-3** document. Select all the content in the document and copy it to the Microsoft Office Clipboard. Paste the copied content into the MOS Formatting message.

❑ Apply the Title style to the first paragraph of the pasted content.

❑ Apply the Subtitle style to the second paragraph.

❑ Format the four paragraphs representing categories of rules as a bulleted list.

❑ Apply the Heading 1 style to the Definitions and General Rules paragraphs.

❑ Apply the Gallery theme to the message and note the changes.

❑ Send the message.

➤ Create a new message to yourself with the subject <u>MOS Links</u>, and do the following:

❑ In the message body, enter the following text: <u>You can find more information about Microsoft Office 2016 here. Please let me know if you have any questions.</u>

❑ Insert a hyperlink from the word *here* that displays the Office website at <u>office.microsoft.com</u> in a new window.

❑ Insert a hyperlink from the words *let me know* that creates an email message addressed to you with the subject <u>Office help request</u>.

❑ Send the message to yourself.

❑ When you receive the message, test the hyperlinks and verify that each performs the expected task.

Objective 2.4: Organize and manage messages

Arrange messages by specific attributes

By default, Outlook displays messages in order by date, from newest to oldest. Alternatively, you can arrange items by any of the following attributes:

- **Account** Messages are grouped by the email account to which they were sent. This is useful if you receive messages for more than one email account in your Inbox (for example, if you receive messages sent to your POP3 account within your Exchange account mailbox).

- **Attachments** Messages are grouped by whether they have attachments and secondarily by date received.

- **Categories** Messages are arranged by the category you assign to them. Messages without a category appear first. Messages with multiple categories assigned to them appear in each of those category groups.

- **Flag: Start Date or Due Date** Unflagged messages and messages without specific schedules appear first. Messages that you've added to your task list with specific start or due dates are grouped by date.

- **From** Messages appear in alphabetical order by the message sender's display name. If you receive messages from a person who uses two different email accounts, or who sends messages from two different email clients (for example, from Outlook and from Windows Mail), the messages will not necessarily be grouped together.

- **Importance** Messages are grouped by priority: High (indicated by a red exclamation point), Normal (the default), or Low (indicated by a blue downward-pointing arrow).

- **To** Messages are grouped alphabetically by the primary recipients (the names or addresses on the To line). The group name exactly reflects the order in which addresses appear on the To line. Therefore, a message addressed to *Bart Duncan; Lukas Keller* is not grouped with a message addressed to *Lukas Keller; Bart Duncan*.

- **Size** Messages are grouped by size of the message, including any attachments. Groups include Huge (1–5 MB), Very Large (500 KB–1 MB), Large (100–500 KB), Medium (25–100 KB), Small (10–25 KB), and Tiny (less than 10 KB). This feature is useful if you work for an organization that limits the size of your Inbox, because you can easily locate large messages and delete them or move them to a personal folder.

- **Subject** Messages are arranged alphabetically by their subjects and then by date. This is similar to arranging by conversation except that the messages aren't threaded.

- **Type** Items in your Inbox (or other folder) are grouped by the type of item—for example, messages, encrypted messages, message receipts, meeting requests and meeting request responses, tasks, Microsoft InfoPath forms, and server notifications.

Tip You can easily sort and group messages by any message settings by choosing that message setting in the Arrange By list.

After arranging the items in your message list, you can change the sort order of the arrangement. The message list header displays the current sort order and arrangement of the message list.

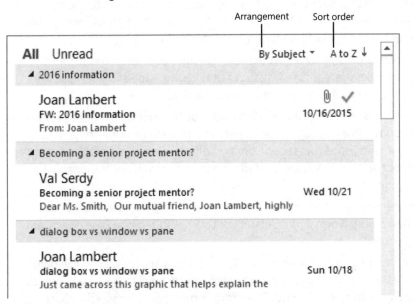

Numbers come before letters when sorting from A to Z

By default, the messages within each arrangement are in groups specific to that category. For example, when messages are arranged by date, they are grouped by date: groups include each day of the current week, Last Week, Two Weeks Ago, Three Weeks Ago, Last Month, and Older. Each group has a header. You can collapse a group so that only the header is visible, or select and process messages by group.

Expanded group   Collapsed groups

All Unread	By Size ▾ Largest ↓
▷ **Large (1 - 5 MB)**	
▷ **Medium (25 KB - 1 MB)**	
◢ **Small (10 - 25 KB)**	

Joan Lambert
Joan Lambert has invited you to 'SBS2016'   10/16/2015
Here's the site that Joan Lambert shared with you.

Jaime Odell
Project schedule   Wed 10/21
Hi Samantha, I'm looking forward to working on the

Susie Carr
Marketing meeting   Wed 10/21
Hi Samantha, I'd like to set up a meeting with you and the

Collapsing groups of messages displays only the group headers

In Single view or Preview view, you can sort messages by any visible column. If you want to sort by an attribute that isn't shown, you can add that column to the view.

To arrange messages by a specific attribute

→ Do one of the following:

- In any view: On the **View** tab, in the **Arrangement** gallery, click the message attribute.

- In Compact view: In the message list header, click the current arrangement, and then click the message attribute.

- In Single view or Preview view: Right-click any column header, click **Arrange By**, and then click the message attribute.

To reverse the sort order of the message list arrangement

→ Do one of the following:

- In any view: On the **View** tab, in the **Arrangement** group, click **Reverse Sort**.

- In Compact view: In the message list header, click the current sort order.

- In Single view or Preview view: Right-click any column header, and then click **Reverse Sort**.

Tip In a list view, you can sort by any column by clicking the column header, and reverse the sort order by clicking the column header again.

To group or ungroup messages

→ Do one of the following:

- In any view: On the **View** tab, in the **Arrangement** gallery, click **Show in Groups**.
- In Compact view: Click the message list header, and then on the menu, click **Show in Groups**.
- In Single view or Preview view: Right-click the header of the column you want to group by, and then click **Group By This Field**.

To select a group of messages

→ Click the group header.

To expand the current message group

→ Do one of the following:

- Click the arrow at the left end of the group header.
- Press the **Right Arrow** key.
- On the **View** tab, in the **Arrangement** group, click **Expand/Collapse**, and then click **Expand This Group**.

To collapse the current message group

→ Do one of the following:

- Click the arrow at the left end of the group header.
- Press the **Left Arrow** key.
- On the **View** tab, in the **Arrangement** group, click **Expand/Collapse**, and then click **Collapse This Group**.

To expand or collapse all message groups

→ On the **View** tab, in the **Arrangement** group, click **Expand/Collapse**, and then click **Expand All Groups** or **Collapse All Groups**.

To reset the message arrangement (and other view settings)

1. On the **View** tab, in the **Current View** group, click **Reset View**.
2. In the **Microsoft Outlook** dialog box prompting you to confirm that you want to reset the current view to its default settings, click **Yes**.

Categorize messages

To help you locate Outlook items associated with a specific subject, project, person, or other attribute, you can create a category specific to that attribute and assign the category to any related items. You can assign a category to any type of Outlook item, such as a message, an appointment, a contact record, or a note. For example, you might assign contact records for customers to a Customers category, or contact records, messages, and meetings associated with a specific project to a category named for the project.

Outlook uses color categories, which combine named categories with color bars to provide an immediate visual cue when you view messages in your Inbox, appointments on your calendar, and other information. Depending on the view of the Outlook items, the category might be indicated by a simple colored block or a large colored bar.

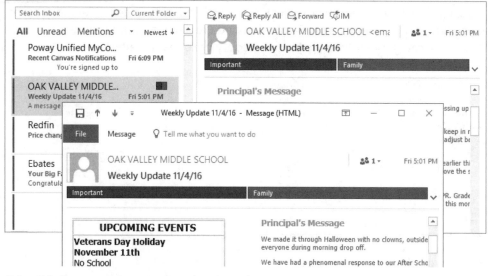

Colored blocks represent the categories assigned to an item

Tip You can locate, sort, and filter Outlook items by category. For information, see "Objective 1.3: Perform search operations in Outlook."

Outlook 2016 has six preconfigured color categories named only by color. You can rename them and create new categories. Each category can have the following elements:

- **Name** The category name can be one simple word or a long, descriptive phrase. The first 32 characters of the category name are visible in the color categories dialog box, but pointing to a truncated name displays the entire name in a ScreenTip.

- **Shortcut key** You can assign any of the 11 available keyboard shortcut combinations (Ctrl+F2 through Ctrl+F12) to the individual color categories. (You can assign only these 11 keyboard shortcuts within the dialog box.)

- **Color** You can assign any of the 25 available colors to a category (or to multiple categories), or you can choose not to assign a color and to rely only on the name to distinguish between categories. (You can't choose colors other than the 25 shown.) When you assign a category that doesn't have an associated color to an Outlook item, the color block or color bar is shown as white.

You can assign an unlimited number of categories to a message, but only the three most recently assigned appear in the message list. The colors representing all the assigned categories appear in the Reading Pane.

Tip If you don't rename a standard color category before assigning it for the first time, Outlook gives you the option of renaming the category the first time you use it.

Outlook users with Exchange, IMAP, or POP accounts can designate one category as the Quick Click category. Outlook assigns the Quick Click category by default when you simply click the Category box or column associated with an item. (Category boxes appear in the message header in Single view and Preview view.) Until you select a Quick Click category, clicking the blank Category boxes has no effect.

Designate your most frequently used category as the Quick Click category

To assign a color category to an item

→ In any mail or contact folder, on the **Categorize** menu, in the **Tags** group on the **Home** tab, click the category you want.

→ In any calendar, on the **Categorize** menu, in the **Tags** group on the tool tab (such as **Appointment** or **Meeting**) that appears for the selected item, click the category you want.

→ In any message list view, click the empty box in the **Categories** column to assign the **Quick Click** category.

Tip You must first set the Quick Click category, as described in the later procedure.

→ In any folder, right-click an item or a selection of items, click **Categorize**, and then click the category you want.

To assign a selected item to multiple color categories

1. On the **Categorize** menu, click **All Categories**.

2. In the **Color Categories** dialog box, select the check boxes of the categories you want to assign, and then click **OK**.

To assign a keyboard shortcut to a color category

1. On the **Categorize** menu, click **All Categories**.
2. In the **Color Categories** dialog box, click the category.
3. In the **Shortcut Key** list, click the key combination you want.
4. In the **Color Categories** dialog box, click **OK**.

To rename a color category

1. On the **Categorize** menu, click **All Categories**.
2. In the **Color Categories** dialog box, do the following, and then click **OK**:
   a. Click the category name, and then click **Rename**.
   b. With the category name selected for editing, enter the name you want, and then press **Enter**.

To create a custom color category

1. On the **Categorize** menu, click **All Categories**.
2. In the **Color Categories** dialog box, click **New**.
3. In the **Add New Category** dialog box, do the following:
   a. In the **Name** box, enter a name for the category.
   b. In the **Color** list, click the color you want to display for the category.
   c. Click the **Shortcut Key** arrow, and then click the keyboard shortcut you want.
4. Click **OK** in each of the open dialog boxes.

To set or change the Quick Click color category

1. Do either of the following to open the Set Quick Click dialog box:
   - On the **Categorize** menu, click **Set Quick Click**.
   - Open the **Outlook Options** dialog box and display the **Advanced** page. In the **Other** section, click **Quick Click**.
2. In the **Set Quick Click** dialog box, select the category you want Outlook to use, and then click **OK**.

Flag messages for follow-up

You can assign a reminder flag for your own reference, to remind you to follow up on a message, contact record, or task. The flags available for messages and tasks are Call, Do Not Forward, Follow Up, For Your Information, Forward, No Response Necessary, Read, Reply, Reply To All, and Review. The flags available for contact records are Follow Up, Call, Arrange Meeting, Send Email, and Send Letter. The default flag for any item is Follow Up. Assigning a flag to an email message or contact record adds it to your task list.

If you add a reminder to a flagged item, Outlook displays the Reminders window at the specified time. From this window, you can dismiss the flag or postpone the reminder.

You can assign a flag to an outgoing message. If you assign a standard flag, it appears only to you. If you specifically flag the message for recipients, Outlook reminds the recipient to follow up on the message with a specific action.

To flag an existing item for follow-up

→ Select the item. On the **Home** tab, in the **Tags** group, click the **Follow Up** button, and then click the flag corresponding to the follow-up time you want to specify.

→ In the message list, right-click the item, point to **Follow Up**, and then click the flag corresponding to the follow-up time you want to specify.

See Also For information about flagging outgoing messages for follow-up, see "Configure message options" in "Objective 2.2: Create messages."

To set a custom flag

1. Select the item. On the **Home** tab, in the **Tags** group, click the **Follow Up** button, and then click **Custom**.
2. In the **Custom** dialog box, in the **Flag to** list, click the flag you want to appear in the item header.
3. Set the start date and due date to control where the item appears on your task list, and then click **OK**.

To add a reminder to a flagged item

1. Do either of the following to open the Custom dialog box and turn on a reminder for the item:
   - Right-click the item, click **Follow Up**, and then click **Add Reminder**.
   - On the **Home** tab, in the **Tags** group, click the **Follow Up** button, and then click **Add Reminder**.
2. With the **Reminder** check box selected, specify the reminder date and time, and then click **OK**.

To flag an outgoing message for your follow-up

→ On the **Message** tab of the message composition window, in the **Tags** group, click the **Follow Up** button, and then click the flag corresponding to the follow-up time you want to specify.

To flag an outgoing message for the recipient's follow-up

1. On the **Message** tab, in the **Tags** group, click the **Follow Up** button, and then click **Custom**.
2. In the **Custom** dialog box, select the **Flag for Recipients** check box.
3. Specify the **Flag to** action and the reminder date and time, and then click **OK**.

Manage conversations

Conversation view is an alternative arrangement of messages grouped by subject. All the messages with the same subject appear together in your Inbox (or other message folder) under one conversation header. You can display differing levels of messages within a conversation. Until you expand the conversation, all the messages grouped within it take up only as much space in your Inbox as a single message would.

Collapsed conversation   Expanded conversation

▷ **Susie Carr; Joan Lambert**   **(2)**
Sample letter for your review   4:35 PM
Sam, is it okay if I get this back to you by Tuesday?

◢ Sample letter for your review   (2)

Susie Carr   4:35 PM
Sam, is it okay if I get this back to you by Tuesday?

Joan Lambert   3:45 PM
Thanks, Samantha! I look forward to your team's

Samantha Smith   *Sent Items*
Whoops, I meant to attach the letter—here it is again.

Samantha Smith   *Sent Items*
Joan, thank you for sending this out for review. I

Joan Lambert   10/17/2015
This is the letter I'm planning to send to the insurance

White right-pointing arrows indicate additional messages collapsed within a conversation

The conversation header provides information about the messages within the conversation, including the number of unread messages and whether one or more messages includes an attachment, is categorized, or is flagged for follow-up.

When you receive a message that is part of a conversation, the entire conversation moves to the top of your Inbox and the new message appears when you click the conversation header. When a conversation includes unread messages, a blue vertical line appears to the left of the header and the conversation subject is in bold blue font, just as an unread message would appear. When you have multiple unread messages, the number is indicated in parentheses following the subject. The senders of the unread messages are listed below the subject.

As with other features of Outlook 2016, you can modify the way Conversation view displays messages to suit the way you work.

Conversation view settings include:

- **Show Messages from Other Folders** By default, Conversation view displays messages stored in any folder, including sent messages that are stored in the Sent Items folder. (Within the expanded conversation, sent messages are indicated by italic font.) You can turn off this setting to display only messages from the current folder.

- **Show Senders Above the Subject** By default, when a conversation is collapsed, the conversation header displays the names of all the conversation participants above the conversation subject; when the conversation is fully expanded, the conversation header displays only the subject. This setting reverses the order of the information in the conversation header; the names of the conversation participants are displayed above the conversation subject. In some cases, such as when Outlook displays a message on the second line, the subject might not be visible at all.

- **Always Expand Selected Conversation** This setting causes Outlook to display all messages in a conversation when you click the Expand Conversation button or conversation header once.

- **Use Classic Indented View** This setting causes Outlook to indent older messages within individual message threads to show the progression of the thread. This setting is not as effective as the default for displaying split conversations because a message might be at the root of multiple branches but can appear only once in the message list.

With Conversation view, you can manage all the messages within a conversation as a group. You can do this by clicking the conversation header to effectively select all the messages in the conversation (they won't appear selected, but, for example, moving the conversation header to another folder moves all the individual messages in the conversation) and then applying your action. Or you can use these conversation-management tools:

- **Ignore Conversation** This command moves the selected conversation and any related messages you receive in the future directly to the Deleted Items folder.

- **Clean Up Conversation** This command deletes redundant messages—whose text is wholly contained within later messages—from a conversation. By default, Outlook doesn't clean up categorized, flagged, or digitally signed messages. You can modify conversation clean-up settings on the Mail page of the Outlook Options dialog box.

To turn Conversation view on or off

➜ On the **View** tab, in the **Messages** group, select or clear the **Show as Conversations** check box.

To select one or more Conversation view options

➜ In the **Messages** group, click **Conversation Settings**, and then click **Show Messages from Other Folders**, **Show Senders Above the Subject**, **Always Expand Selected Conversation**, or **Use Classic Indented View**.

To expand a conversation

➜ Click the conversation header or the **Expand Conversation** button to the left of the conversation header once to display the most recent message in the Reading Pane and to display all the unique messages in the conversation.

➜ Click the **Expand Conversation** button twice to display all messages in the conversation, including messages from your Sent Items folder.

To clean up a conversation

1. Select one or more messages or conversations.
2. On the **Home** tab, in the **Delete** group, click the **Clean Up** button.
3. In the **Clean Up** list, do one of the following:
   - To delete all redundant messages from the selected conversations, click **Clean Up Conversation** and then, in the **Clean Up Conversation** dialog box, click **Clean Up**.
   - To delete all redundant messages from the current folder but not its subfolders, click **Clean Up Folder** and then, in the **Clean Up Folder** dialog box, click **Clean Up Folder**.
   - To delete all redundant messages from the current folder and its subfolders, click **Clean Up Folder & Subfolders** and then, in the **Clean Up Folder** dialog box, click **Clean Up Folder**.

To ignore a conversation

➜ Press **Ctrl+Del** to ignore the currently active conversation.

Or

1. Select one or more messages or conversations.
2. On the **Home** tab, in the **Delete** group, click the **Ignore** button.
3. In the **Ignore Conversation** dialog box, click **Ignore Conversation**.

Organize messages in folders

You can create folders to contain email messages, calendar information, contact records, and other items. You must specify the type of items the folder will contain when you create it.

To create a message folder

→ In the **Folder Pane**, right-click the parent folder (usually the Inbox), and then click **New Folder**. Enter the folder name in the subfolder name area that opens, and then press **Enter**.

Or

1. On the **Folder** tab, in the **New** group, click **New Folder**.

2. In the **Create New Folder** dialog box, enter a name for the folder in the **Name** box, and then in the **Folder contains** list, click **Mail and Post Items**.

3. In the **Select where to place the folder** list, click the location in which you want to create the folder (usually the Inbox).

4. In the **Create New Folder** dialog box, click **OK**.

To move selected messages and create a message folder

1. Do either of the following:

   • Right-click the messages, and then click **Move**.

   • On the **Home** tab, in the **Move** group, click **Move**.

2. In the lower section of the list, click **Other Folder**.

3. In the **Move Items** dialog box, click **New**.

4. In the **Create New Folder** dialog box, enter a name for the folder in the **Name** box, and then in the **Folder contains** list, click **Mail and Post Items**.

5. In the **Select where to place the folder** list, click the location in which you want to create the folder (usually the Inbox).

6. Click **OK** in each of the open dialog boxes.

To move selected messages to an existing folder

→ Drag the messages from the message list to the destination folder in the **Folder Pane**.

Or

1. Do either of the following:
   - Right-click the messages, and then click **Move**.
   - On the **Home** tab, in the **Move** group, click **Move**.
2. Do either of the following:
   - In the upper section of the list, click the destination folder.
   - In the lower section of the list, click **Other Folder**. In the **Move Items** dialog box, click the folder to which you want to move the messages, and then click **OK**.

Create and manage Quick Steps

With the Quick Steps feature, you can perform multiple processes on one or more email messages with only one click. For example, you can reply to an email message and delete the original message, or flag a message for follow-up and move it to a specific folder. Quick Steps are somewhat like rules, but you must initiate them manually.

A default Outlook installation includes these five Quick Steps:

- **Move to** Moves the selected message to a folder that you specify the first time you use the Quick Step and marks the message as read. After you specify the folder, the Quick Step name changes to include the folder name.

- **To Manager** Forwards the selected message to a person or people you specify the first time you use the Quick Step. You can edit the Quick Step to include Cc and Bcc recipients, a specific message subject, a follow-up flag, a level of importance, and specific message text, and to send the message one minute after you click the Quick Step command.

- **Team Email** Creates a message to a person or people you specify the first time you use the Quick Step. You can edit the Quick Step to include Cc and Bcc recipients, a specific message subject, a follow-up flag, a level of importance, and specific message text, and to send the message one minute after you click the Quick Step command.

- **Done** Moves the selected message to a folder that you specify the first time you use the Quick Step, marks the message as read, and marks the message as complete so that a check mark is displayed in the follow-up flag location.

- **Reply & Delete** Creates a response to the original message sender and immediately deletes the original message.

2

Quick Steps are available from the Quick Steps group on the Home tab of the Mail module, and from the shortcut menu that appears when you right-click a message or group of messages.

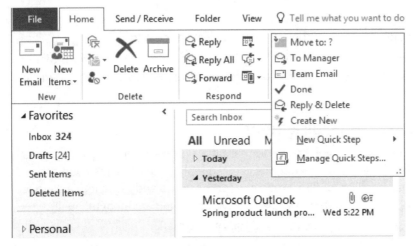

Outlook provides several built-in Quick Steps that perform common tasks

For each of the built-in Quick Steps, you can change its name; edit, add, and remove actions; and specify tooltip text that appears when you point to the Quick Step in the Quick Steps gallery.

You can create your own Quick Steps that include any combination of up to 12 actions. You can base a new Quick Step on a standard set of actions or an existing Quick Step, or create it from scratch. You can assign shortcut keys (Ctrl+Shift+1 through Ctrl+Shift+9) to up to nine Quick Steps.

Tip The Quick Steps feature is available only in the Mail module. If you connect to multiple accounts, the Quick Steps in each Mail module are specific to that account.

Edit Quick Step   ?   X

> _N_ame:
>
> Complete Flagged Message
>
> Edit the actions the quick step performs.
>
> Actions ─────────────────────────
>
> Move to folder   ⌄   X
>
>   Completed   ⌄
>
> Clear flags on message   ⌄   X
>
> ! Set importance   ⌄   X
>
>   Importance: Normal   ⌄
>
> Mark as read   ⌄   X
>
> ───────────────────────────
>
> _A_dd Action
>
> Optional ─────────────────────────
>
> _S_hortcut key: Choose a shortcut ⌄
>
> _T_ooltip text: Use this after you complete the task associated with a message that is flagged for follow up.
>
>   _S_ave   Cancel

Perform up to 12 actions by using a Quick Step

To set up and use an existing Quick Step

1. On the **Home** tab, in the **Quick Steps** gallery, click the Quick Step you want to perform.

2. In the **First Time Setup** dialog box, do either of the following:

   - Provide the information required for the selected command, and then click **Save**.

   - In the **First Time Setup** dialog box, provide the information required for the selected command, click **Options**, and then follow the instructions for changing the properties of an existing Quick Step.

To perform an existing Quick Step

1. Select a message or group of messages.
2. Do either of the following:
   - On the **Home** tab, in the **Quick Steps** gallery, click the Quick Step you want to perform.
   - Right-click the selection, point to **Quick Steps**, and then click the Quick Step you want to perform.

To display the properties of an existing Quick Step

1. On the **Home** tab, click the **Quick Steps** dialog box launcher.
2. In the **Manage Quick Steps** dialog box, in the **Quick step** list, click the Quick Step you want to view.

To change the properties of an existing Quick Step

1. Do either of the following:
   - In the **Quick Steps** gallery, right-click the Quick Step you want to modify, and then click **Edit** *Quick Step name*.
   - On the **Home** tab, click the **Quick Steps** dialog box launcher. In the **Manage Quick Steps** dialog box, click the Quick Step you want to modify, and then click **Edit**.
2. In the **Edit Quick Step** dialog box, do any of the following, and then click **Save**:
   - To rename the Quick Step, replace the text in the **Name** box.
   - To replace an action, in the **Actions** list, click the existing action, and then click the replacement action. Supply any secondary information necessary for the replacement action.
   - To add an action, click **Add Action**. Click **Choose an Action**, and then click the action you want to add. Supply any secondary information necessary for the new action.
   - To assign a shortcut key combination to the Quick Step, in the **Shortcut key** list, click the key combination you want.
   - To change the message that appears when you point to the Quick Step, edit the text in the **Tooltip text** box.

To create a Quick Step

1. Do one of the following:

   - In the **Quick Steps** gallery, click **Create New** to begin creating a custom Quick Step.

   - Expand the **Quick Steps** gallery, click **New Quick Step**, and then click the basic action set you want the Quick Step to perform, or click **Custom**.

   - Click the **Quick Steps** dialog box launcher. In the **Manage Quick Steps** dialog box, do either of the following:

     ○ Click **New**. Then click the basic action set you want the Quick Step to perform, or click **Custom**.

     ○ In the **Quick step** list, click an existing Quick Step on which you want to base the new Quick Step, and then click **Duplicate**.

2. In the **First Time Setup** or **Edit Quick Step** dialog box, provide the necessary information, and then click **Finish**.

To reset a built-in Quick Step

1. On the **Home** tab, click the **Quick Steps** dialog box launcher.

2. In the **Manage Quick Steps** dialog box, in the **Quick step** list, click the Quick Step you want to reset.

3. Click **Reset to Defaults**, and then click **Yes** in the **Microsoft Outlook** dialog box that opens.

To delete a Quick Step

→ In the **Quick Steps** gallery, right-click the Quick Step, and then click **Delete**.

→ Click the **Quick Steps** dialog box launcher. In the **Manage Quick Steps** dialog box, click the Quick Step you want to delete, and then click **Delete**.

Configure basic AutoArchive settings

From the AutoArchive section of the Advanced page of the Outlook Options dialog box, you can open the AutoArchive dialog box. In this dialog box, you can configure automatic archival operations separate from those that might be managed by your organization's Exchange administrator. The AutoArchive feature is turned off by default.

You can specify item archiving options and upcoming appointment reminder options

To automatically archive items

1. Open the **Outlook Options** dialog box and display the **Advanced** page.

2. In the **AutoArchive** section, click **AutoArchive Settings**.

3. In the **AutoArchive** dialog box, do the following:

   a. Select the **Run AutoArchive every** check box.

   b. In the adjacent **days** box, enter or select the frequency.

   c. In the **During AutoArchive** section, review the options and configure the settings to meet your needs.

4. Click **OK** in the open dialog boxes.

Delegate access

You can delegate control of one or more Outlook modules to a co-worker so that person can create messages, appointments, tasks, contact records, and notes, and respond to requests on your behalf.

When delegating access, you can assign specific permission levels for each module. Permission options include the following:

- **None** The delegate cannot read, create, or modify items in the module.
- **Reviewer** The delegate can read items in the module, but cannot create or modify items.
- **Author** The delegate can read and create items in the module, but cannot modify existing items.
- **Editor** The delegate can read, create, and modify items in the module.

When delegating permissions, the default settings give the delegate Editor permissions to the Calendar and Tasks modules only. However, you can also delegate permission to your Inbox, Contacts module, and Notes module.

> **Tip** When you delegate permissions to your calendar, you can specify whether meeting requests are sent only to you, only to your delegates, or to both you and your delegates.

Delegate Permissions: Susie Carr ✕

This delegate has the following permissions

| | Calendar | Editor (can read, create, and modify items) ⌄ |

☑ Delegate receives copies of meeting-related messages sent to me

| | Tasks | Editor (can read, create, and modify items) ⌄ |

| | Inbox | None ⌄ |

None
Reviewer (can read items)
Author (can read and create items)
Editor (can read, create, and modify items)

| | Contacts | |

| | Notes | None ⌄ |

☐ Automatically send a message to delegate summarizing these permissions
☐ Delegate can see my private items

OK   Cancel

Stipulate delegated permissions individually for each module

To delegate control of your account to another Outlook user

1. On the **Info** page of the Backstage view, click **Account Settings**, and then click **Delegate Access**.

2. In the **Delegates** dialog box, click **Add**.

3. In the **Add Users** dialog box, click the person you want to delegate control to, click **Add**, and then click **OK**.

4. In the **Delegate Permissions** dialog box, set the permission level you want the delegate to have for each module.

5. If you want to inform your delegate about the permission he or she has to your account, select the **Automatically send a message...** check box.

6. If you want to allow your delegate to view details of items that you mark as private, select the **Delegate can see my private items** check box.

7. In the **Delegate Permissions** dialog box, click **OK**.

To modify delegation permissions

1. On the **Info** page of the Backstage view, click **Account Settings**, and then click **Delegate Access**.

2. In the **Delegates** dialog box, select the delegate, and then click **Permissions**.

3. In the **Delegate Permissions** dialog box, set the permission level you want the delegate to have for each module, select any additional options, and then click **OK**.

To rescind a delegation

1. On the **Info** page of the Backstage view, click **Account Settings**, and then click **Delegate Access**.

2. In the **Delegates** dialog box, select the delegate, click **Remove**, and then click **OK**.

Objective 2.4 practice tasks

There are no practice files for these tasks. Before you begin, alert two colleagues that you're going to practice working with Quick Steps.

➤ Display your Outlook Inbox and do the following:

❑ Arrange the messages in your Inbox by subject and sort them from Z to A.

❑ Create a subfolder of your Inbox named <u>Important</u>.

❑ Set up the built-in Team Email Quick Step to send a message with the subject <u>MOS Certification Information</u> to you and two other people.

❑ Specify that Outlook should prefill the message body with the text <u>New information about MOS certification</u>.

➤ Create a Quick Step named <u>Categorize MOS</u> that does the following:

❑ Assigns the message to a category named <u>MOS Study Guide</u>. (Create the category during the process of creating the Quick Step. Configure the category to use the orange color, and assign the keyboard shortcut Ctrl+F2.)

❑ Creates a task containing the text of the message.

➤ Run the Team Email Quick Step and do the following:

❑ In the message, replace the built-in message body content with the text <u>I'm testing Outlook Quick Steps; please reply to this message.</u>

❑ Send the message.

➤ After you receive the two responses to the MOS Certification Information message, do the following:

❑ Select the two messages and run the Categorize MOS Quick Step.

❑ Flag one of the messages for follow-up tomorrow.

❑ Manually assign the MOS Study Guide category to one additional message.

❑ Search your mailbox to locate all items assigned to the MOS Study Guide category. Move the items to the Important folder.

➤ Display the contents of your Inbox in Conversation view and do the following:

❑ Arrange the messages by conversation.

❑ Identify a conversation with multiple threads, and clean up the conversation by using the Clean Up command.

Objective group 3
Manage schedules

The skills tested in this section of the Microsoft Office Specialist exam for Microsoft Outlook 2016 relate to managing calendars, calendar items, tasks, and notes. Specifically, the following objectives are associated with this set of skills:

3.1 Create and manage calendars

3.2 Create appointments, meetings, and events

3.3 Organize and manage appointments, meetings, and events

3.4 Create and manage notes and tasks

Actively using the Outlook calendar is a big step toward efficient time management. You can track appointments and events, organize meetings, and schedule time to complete tasks. The Outlook calendar differentiates between working and nonworking time so that your calendar correctly indicates times that you're available for meetings. You can specify your standard working days and times, track your schedule in multiple time zones, and smoothly switch between time zones when you travel.

In addition to your primary Outlook calendar, you can create, import, link to, subscribe to, and manage other calendars within the Calendar module. You can share a calendar or selected information from it with people inside or outside of your organization.

Outlook provides other modules in which to track information. The Tasks module provides a way to track independent tasks and messages that you want to follow-up on, and to assign tasks to other people. You can display your daily task lists in the calendar to coordinate the time required to complete them, and you can save general information in the Notes module.

This chapter guides you in studying ways of managing calendars, appointments, meetings, and events; tracking tasks; and recording information in notes.

> To complete the practice tasks in this chapter, you need the practice file contained in the **MOSOutlook2016\Objective3** practice file folder. For more information, see "Download the practice files" in this book's introduction.

Objective 3.1: Create and manage calendars

Configure calendar settings

The Calendar module offers four distinct views of content. These views are:

- **Calendar** This is the standard view in which you display your Outlook calendar. In the Day, Work Week, or Week arrangement, Calendar view displays the subject, location, and organizer (if space allows) of each appointment, meeting, or event, in addition to the availability bar and any special icons, such as *Private* or *Recurrence*.

- **Preview** In the Day, Work Week, or Week arrangement, this view displays additional information, including information from the notes area of the appointment window, as space allows.

- **List** This list view displays all appointments, meetings, and events on your calendar.

- **Active** This list view displays only future appointments, meetings, and events.

In your Outlook calendar, the time that you indicate you are available for other people to schedule meetings with you is referred to as your *work week*. The calendar time slots within your work week are colored differently from those outside of your work week, and are the only time slots made available to people on your network when they are searching for a time to meet with you.

By default, the Outlook work week is defined as from 8:00 A.M. to 5:00 P.M. (in your local time zone), Monday through Friday. You can change this to match your individual work schedule. In Outlook 2016, you can specify a start time and end time for your standard work day, specify the days of the week that you work, and specify the day of the week that you'd like to appear first when you display only the work week in your calendar.

Tip Outlook doesn't allow you to define a workday that crosses midnight or to define different start and end times for different days.

If you frequently travel or work with colleagues or clients outside of your usual time zone, you might want to change the time zone on your computer so that information such as the receipt time of email messages, appointment times, and the time on the clock in the Windows Taskbar notification area reflects your current location. If you have appointments in both time zones, you can display both time zones on the left side of the Calendar pane, and swap between zones when you travel. That way, you can be sure to correctly enter appointments at the time they will occur in their respective time zones.

Working time   Nonworking time

Working and nonworking time in Work Week view

To display a different calendar view

→ On the **View** tab, in the **Current View** group, click **Change View**, and then click **Calendar**, **Preview**, **List**, or **Active**.

To modify the time period shown in Calendar view or Preview view

→ In the **Arrange** group on the **Home** tab, or in the **Arrangement** group on the **View** tab, click **Day**, **Work Week**, **Week**, **Month** or **Schedule View**.

→ On the **Home** tab, in the **Go To** group, click **Today** or **Next 7 Days**.

To modify the time segments shown on the calendar

→ On the **View** tab, in the **Arrangement** group, click **Time Scale**, and then click **60 Minutes**, **30 Minutes**, **15 Minutes**, **10 Minutes**, **6 Minutes**, or **5 Minutes**.

To modify the grouping of calendar items in List view or Active view

→ On the **View** tab, in the **Arrangement** gallery, click **Categories**, **Start Date**, **Recurrence**, or **Location**.

→ Right-click any column heading, and then click **Group By This Field**.

To sort calendar items in List view or Active view

→ Click any column heading to sort by the values in that column.

→ Click the active sort column heading to reverse the sort order.

→ On the **View** tab, in the **Arrangement** group, click **Reverse Sort**.

To set work times on the default calendar

1. Open the **Outlook Options** dialog box and display the **Calendar** page.

2. In the **Work time** section, do any of the following:

   • Set the start time and end time of the work day you want to define.

   • In the **Work week** area, select the check boxes of the days you want to include in your work week.

   • In the **First day of week** list, click the day you want to appear first (on the left) in the Work Week view of your calendar.

   • In the **First week of year** list, click **Starts on Jan 1**, **First 4-day week**, or **First full week**.

3. In the **Outlook Options** dialog box, click **OK** to save the changes.

To change the calendar time zone

1. Open the **Outlook Options** dialog box and display the **Calendar** page.

2. In the **Time zones** section, do the following:

   a. Click the **Time zone** list, and then click the time zone you want to display.

   b. In the corresponding **Label** box, enter a description of up to 32 characters.

3. In the **Outlook Options** dialog box, click **OK** to save the changes.

To display multiple time zones

1. Open the **Outlook Options** dialog box and display the **Calendar** page.

2. In the **Time zones** section, do the following:

   a. Select the **Show a second time zone** check box.

   b. In the corresponding **Time zone** list, click the second time zone you want to display.

   c. In the corresponding **Label** box, enter a description of up to 32 characters.

3. In the **Outlook Options** dialog box, click **OK** to save the changes.

To switch your calendar between the primary and secondary time zones

1. Open the **Outlook Options** dialog box and display the **Calendar** page.

2. In the **Time zones** section, click the **Swap Time Zones** button.

3. In the **Outlook Options** dialog box, click **OK** to save the changes.

Work with multiple calendars

The Calendar button on the Navigation Bar links to the calendar of your default email account. You can also display the following types of calendars in the Calendar module:

- **Calendars of your other email accounts** These are available automatically when you configure Outlook to connect to an account.
- **Custom calendars** You create a calendar in the same way that you do a folder that contains mail, contact records, or other items.
- **Calendars of people within your organization** Within an organization that uses Microsoft Exchange Server, you can display the availability of your co-workers, individually or in a group, without special permission.
- **Shared calendars** Other Outlook users can share their calendars with you.
- **SharePoint site calendars** You can connect a SharePoint calendar to Outlook.
- **Internet calendars** You can subscribe to or import calendars from the Internet.

All these types of calendars are available to you from the Folder Pane in the Calendar module or the Folder List in the Mail module.

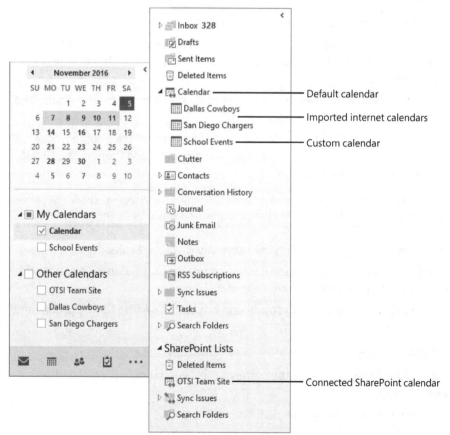

Accessing calendars from the Folder Pane

You can display calendars individually, or you can display more than one calendar at a time. For example, you might have separate business and personal calendars and want to view them together. You can view multiple calendars next to each other, or you can overlay them to display a composite view of the separate calendars. When you view and scroll through multiple calendars, they all display the same date or time period.

To display or hide multiple calendars

→ In the **Folder Pane** of the Calendar module, select or clear the check box of individual calendars.

→ In the **Folder Pane** of the Mail module, expand the **Folder List**, and then click a calendar to display it.

To create a secondary calendar

1. Display the Calendar module. On the **Folder** tab, in the **New** group, click **New Calendar**.

2. In the **Create New Folder** dialog box, name the calendar, select its location, and then click **OK**.

To create a calendar group by choosing group members

1. Display the Calendar module in Calendar view. On the **Home** tab, in the **Manage Calendars** group, click **Calendar Groups** and then, in the list, click **Create New Calendar Group**.

2. In the **Create New Calendar Group** dialog box, enter a name for the group, and then click **OK**.

3. In the **Select Name** dialog box, double-click the names of the people whose calendars you want to include in the calendar group to add them to the **Group Members** box, and then click **OK**.

Tip You can display an up-to-date group schedule at any time by selecting the check box of the calendar group in the Folder Pane. You can hide the group schedule by clearing the check box.

To create a calendar group containing the currently displayed calendars

1. On the **Home** tab, in the **Manage Calendars** group, click **Calendar Groups** and then, in the list, click **Save as New Calendar Group**.

2. In the **Create New Calendar Group** dialog box, enter a name for the group, and then click **OK**.

To delete a calendar group

1. In the **Folder Pane**, right-click the name of the calendar group, and then click **Delete Group**.

2. In the confirmation dialog box, click **Yes**.

To delete a calendar from the Calendar module or from a calendar group

→ In the **Folder Pane**, right-click the calendar name, and then click **Delete Calendar**.

To switch between Overlay Mode and Side-By-Side Mode

→ On the title bar tab of any secondary calendar, click the **View in Overlay Mode** button (the left-pointing ← arrow). In Overlay Mode, click either calendar tab to display that calendar on top of the other calendar.

→ On any overlaid calendar, click the **View in Side-By-Side Mode** button (the right-pointing → arrow) to return to the standard display.

→ On the **View** tab, in the **Arrangement** group, click **Overlay** to turn Overlay Mode on or off for the active calendar.

→ Right-click any calendar tab, and then click **Overlay** to turn Overlay Mode on or off for that calendar.

Share calendar information

Co-workers can view your available working time when they schedule meetings with you or view your calendar through Outlook. If you want to share more information with co-workers or with people outside of your organization, you have several options for doing so.

- You can allow selected co-workers to view calendar item details by sharing the calendar with them.

- You can allow selected co-workers to view your entire calendar and to make appointments and respond to meeting requests on your behalf by delegating control of the calendar to them.

- You can publish your calendar to the Office.com website or to a corporate web server and then share the published calendar with any person who has access to the Internet.

- You can send a professional graphic representation of your appointments during a selected date range by email to any person who uses an HTML-capable email program (not only people who use Outlook), including colleagues, friends, and family members.

The options for sending, sharing, and publishing calendar information are available from the Share group on the Home tab of the Calendar module.

See Also For information about delegating access to your calendar, see "Delegate access" in "Objective 2.4: "Organize and manage messages."

If your email address is part of an Exchange network, you can give permission to other people on your network to view, modify, or create items within a calendar or any other type of Outlook folder. The level of access each co-worker has is governed by the permissions you assign to him or her. Using this method, you can share your default calendar or a secondary calendar that you create, import, or subscribe to.

Shared calendars are available from the Folder Pane of the Calendar module

After you share a calendar, you can specify the actions each person with whom you share the calendar can take. You can select a permission level, which includes Read, Write, Delete, and other settings, or you can select individual settings in each category.

Tip From the Permissions page, you can change the default permission level to your calendar and permit co-workers to view more information than only your availability.

Calendar Properties ✕

General | Home Page | AutoArchive | **Permissions** | Synchronization

Name	Permission Level
Default	Free/Busy time
Anonymous	None
Samantha Smith	Custom

Add... | Remove | Properties...

Permissions

Permission Level: [⌄]

Read
- ○ None
- ○ Free/Busy tim
- ⊙ Free/Busy tim subject, locati
- ○ Full Details

Other Free/Bus

Owner
Publishing Editor
Editor
Publishing Author
Author
Nonediting Author
Reviewer
Contributor
Free/Busy time, subject, location
Free/Busy time

Delete items
- ⊙ None
- ○ Own
- ○ All

Other
- ☐ Folder owner
- ☐ Folder contact
- ☑ Folder visible

OK | Cancel | Apply

3

You can specify the level of detail and actions available to each person you share your calendar with

To share a calendar

1. In the Calendar module, display the calendar you want to share.

2. On the **Home** tab, in the **Share** group, click **Share Calendar** to create a sharing invitation.

3. Address the invitation to the person with whom you'd like to share your calendar. If you'd like to request that the person reciprocate by sharing his or her calendar with you, select the **Request permission to view recipient's Calendar** check box.

4. In the **Details** list, click the level of detail you want to share: **Availability only**, **Limited details**, or **Full details**.

5. Add any notes you want to in the content pane, send the message, and then click **Yes** in the **Microsoft Outlook** dialog box that asks you to confirm that you want to share the calendar with the specified permissions.

To configure permissions for a shared calendar

1. On the **Home** tab, in the **Share** group, click **Calendar Permissions**.

2. On the **Permissions** tab of the **Calendar Properties** dialog box, do either of the following, and then click **OK**:

   - Click a preconfigured permission level in the **Permission Level** list.
   - Select individual options.

Objective 3.1 practice tasks

There are no practice files for these tasks. Before you begin, alert a colleague that you are going to practice sharing your calendar.

➤ Display the following views of your primary calendar:

❑ Display the calendar for next month.

❑ Display only the second week of the month.

❑ Display only the fifteenth day of the month.

➤ Configure your Outlook options as follows:

❑ Set your work week to Tuesday through Friday, from 10:00 A.M. to 6:00 P.M.

❑ Add a time zone to your calendar. Choose a time zone that is two hours ahead of your local time zone.

➤ Return to your primary calendar and do the following:

❑ Use the Go To command to display the calendar for today.

❑ Change the time scale to divide the calendar into 15-minute intervals.

➤ Create a secondary calendar named MOS Schedule, and display it beside your primary calendar.

➤ Create a calendar group named MOS Team that includes the secondary calendar and the calendar of a colleague, and do the following:

❑ Display the calendar group in Schedule view.

❑ Display the calendar group in Overlay Mode.

❑ Hide (but don't delete) the calendar group.

➤ Share the MOS Schedule calendar with a colleague as follows:

❑ Configure the invitation to display your availability but not the details of appointments, meetings, and events on your calendar.

❑ Request that your colleague share his or her calendar with you.

❑ Send the invitation.

Objective 3.2:
Create appointments, meetings, and events

Create appointments and events

Appointments are blocks of time you schedule for only yourself (as opposed to meet-ings, to which you invite other people). An appointment has a specific start time and end time.

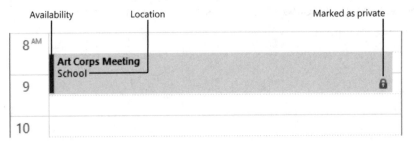

A typical appointment window

Events occur for one or more 24-hour days—for example, a birthday, a vacation week, or anything else occurring on specific days but not beginning and ending at specific times. In all other respects, creating an event is identical to creating an appointment, in that you can specify a location, indicate recurrence, indicate your availability, and attach additional information to the event item.

You can schedule a simple appointment or event directly on the calendar, or provide additional details in an appointment window. The minimum requirements are the sub-ject and the a time. You can also include the appointment location, and enter ancillary information (including formatted text, website links, and even file attachments) in the notes area so that it is readily available to you at the time of the appointment.

Appointment details available in Day view

When creating an appointment, meeting, or event, you indicate your availability (also referred to as *Free/Busy time*) by marking it as Free, Working Elsewhere, Tentative, Busy, or Out Of Office. The appointment time is color-coded on your calendar to match the availability you indicate. Your availability is visible to other Outlook users on your network, and is also displayed when you share your calendar or send calendar information to other people.

To create a simple appointment with the default settings

1. In the Calendar module, display the date on which you want to schedule the appointment.

2. In the **Calendar** pane, click the desired time slot or drag through consecutive time slots.

3. Enter the information you want to appear as the appointment subject, and then press **Enter**.

To open a new appointment window

→ In the **Calendar** pane, right-click the desired time slot or drag through consecutive time slots and right-click the selection, and then click **New Appointment**.

→ In the Calendar module, on the **Home** tab, in the **New** group, click **New Appointment**.

→ In the Calendar module, press **Ctrl+N**.

→ In any module, on the **Home** tab, in the **New** group, click **New Items**, and then click **Appointment**.

→ In any module, press **Ctrl+Shift+A**.

To create an appointment with custom settings

1. Open a new appointment window.

2. In the appointment window, enter the information you want to appear on the calendar in the **Subject** and **Location** boxes.

3. Click or enter the appointment start date in the left **Start time** list and, if the appointment extends across multiple days, click or enter the appointment end date in the left **End time** list.

4. Click or enter the appointment start time in the right **Start time** list and the appointment end time in the right **End time** list.

5. On the **Appointment** tab, in the **Options** group, click your availability during the specified appointment time—**Free, Working Elsewhere, Tentative, Busy**, or **Out of Office**—in the **Show As** list.

6. In the **Options** group, in the **Reminder** list, click the length of time prior to the appointment (or **None**) when you would like Outlook to display a reminder.

7. On the **Appointment** tab, in the **Actions** group, click **Save & Close**.

3

To create an appointment from an email message

1. In the Mail module, drag the message from the **Mail** pane to the **Calendar** button on the **Navigation Bar**.

2. In the appointment window that opens, edit the appointment details as necessary.

3. On the **Appointment** tab, in the **Actions** group, click **Save & Close**.

To create an event with default settings

1. Display the calendar in Day view, Work Week view, Week view, or Month view.

2. In the **Calendar** pane, click the space that contains the date (in views other than Month view, the space below the day header and above the time slots).

3. Enter the event name, and then press **Enter**.

To create an event with custom settings

→ In an appointment window header, to the right of the **Start time** boxes, select the **All day event** check box.

Create meetings

A primary difficulty when scheduling a meeting is finding a time that works for all the people who need to attend it. Scheduling meetings through Outlook is significantly simpler than other methods of scheduling meetings, particularly when you need to accommodate the schedules of several people. Outlook displays the individual and collective schedules of people within your own organization, and of people outside of your organization who have published their calendars to the Internet. You can review attendees' schedules to locate a time when everyone is available, or have Outlook find a convenient time for you.

You can send an Outlook meeting invitation (referred to as a *meeting request*) to any person who has an email account—even to a person who doesn't use Outlook. You can send a meeting request from any type of email account (such as an Exchange account or an Internet email account).

The meeting window has two pages: the Appointment page and the Scheduling Assistant page. The Appointment page is visible by default. You can enter all the required information directly on the Appointment page, or use the additional features available on the Scheduling Assistant page to find the best time for the meeting.

The Appointment page of a meeting window

The Room Finder is open by default on the right side of each page of the meeting window. This handy tool helps you to identify dates and times that work for the greatest number of attendees, in addition to available locations. The monthly calendar at the top of the Room Finder indicates the collective availability of the group on each day, as follows:

- Dates that occur in the past and nonworking days are gray.
- Days when all attendees are available are white (Good).
- Days when most attendees are available are light blue (Fair).
- Days when most attendees are not available are medium blue (Poor).

Tip All the capabilities for the Room Finder are available for Exchange accounts, but functionality is limited for other types of accounts. You can display or hide the Room Finder page by clicking Room Finder in the Options group on the Meeting tab.

Managed conference rooms that are available at the indicated meeting time are shown in the center of the Room Finder. At the bottom of the Room Finder, the Suggested Times list displays attendee availability for appointments of the length of time you have specified for the meeting.

People you invite to meetings are referred to as *attendees*. By default, the attendance of each attendee is indicated as Required. You can inform noncritical attendees of the meeting by marking their attendance as Optional. You can invite entire groups of people by using a contact group or distribution list. You can also invite managed resources, such as conference rooms and audio/visual equipment, that have been set up by your organization's Exchange administrator.

A meeting request should have at least one attendee other than you, and must have a start time and an end time. It should also include a subject and a location, but Outlook will send the meeting request without this information if you specifically allow it. The body of a meeting request can include text and web links, and you can also attach files. This is a convenient way to distribute meeting information to attendees ahead of time.

The secondary page of the meeting window is the Scheduling Assistant page, if your email account is part of an Exchange Server network. Otherwise, the secondary page is the Scheduling page, which doesn't include the Room Finder feature.

The Scheduling Assistant page of a meeting window

The Scheduling and Scheduling Assistant pages include a group schedule that shows the status of each attendee's time throughout your working day. Outlook indicates your suggested meeting time on the group schedule. If free/busy information is available for meeting attendees, the status is indicated by the standard free/busy colors and patterns that match the legend at the bottom of the page. If no information is available (either because Outlook can't connect to an attendee's calendar or because the proposed meeting is further out than the scheduling information stored on the server), Outlook shows the time with gray diagonal stripes. The row at the top of the schedule, to the right of the All Attendees heading, indicates the collective schedule of all the attendees.

To open a new meeting window

→ In the Calendar module, on the **Home** tab, in the **New** group, click **New Meeting**.

→ In any module, do either of the following:

- On the **Home** tab, in the **New** group, click **New Items**, and then click **Meeting**.
- Press **Ctrl+Shift+Q**.

To create a meeting from an email message

→ In the message reading window, do either of the following:

- On the **Message** tab, in the **Respond** group, click the **Reply with Meeting** button.
- Press **Ctrl+Alt+R**.

To create a meeting from an appointment or event

→ In an appointment or event window, on the item-specific tab, do either of the following:

- In the **Attendees** group, click **Invite Attendees**.
- In the **Show** group, click **Scheduling Assistant**.

To invite attendees and schedule resources

→ On the **Appointment** page of the meeting window, enter the email addresses or names of the attendees or resources in the **To** box.

→ On the **Scheduling** or **Scheduling Assistant** page of the meeting window, enter the email addresses or names of the attendees and resources in the **All Attendees** list.

Or

1. On the **Appointment** page of the meeting window, click the **To** button.
2. In the **Select Attendees and Resources** dialog box, locate and double-click the contacts and managed resources you want to invite, and then click **OK**.

To invite optional attendees

1.   Invite the attendee by using any of the previously discussed methods.

2.   On the **Meeting** tab, in the **Show** group, click **Scheduling Assistant**.

3.   In the **All Attendees** list, click the icon immediately to the left of the optional attendee's name and then, in the list, click **Optional Attendee**.

To use the Room Finder

→   To display suggested meeting times, click a date in the **Date Navigator** at the top of the **Room Finder** pane.

→   To update the meeting request, click a meeting time in the **Suggested Times** list.

Manage calendar items

If you have the same appointment on a regular basis—for example, a bimonthly haircut or a weekly exercise class—you can set it up in your Outlook calendar as a *recurring appointment*. A recurring appointment can happen at almost any regular interval, such as every Tuesday and Thursday, every other week, or the last day of every month. Configuring an appointment recurrence creates multiple instances of the appointment in your calendar at the time interval you specify. You can set the appointment to recur until further notice, to end after a certain number of occurrences, or to end by a certain date. The individual appointments are linked. When making changes to a recurring appointment, you can choose to update all occurrences or only an individual occurrence of the appointment.

You can configure recurrence at any regular interval

To configure recurrence for calendar items

1. Do either of the following:

   - On the item-specific tab of the item window, in the **Options** group, click **Recurrence**.

   - In the **Calendar** pane, select the calendar item. On the item-specific tool tab, in the **Options** group, click **Recurrence**.

2. In the **Appointment Recurrence** dialog box, do the following, and then click **OK**:

   a. In the **Recurrence pattern** area, click a frequency option.

   b. In the adjacent area, which changes according to the frequency option you select, adjust the settings to reflect the recurrence you want.

   c. In the **Range of recurrence** area, select the appropriate end date for the series of appointments or events.

To change the time of an existing calendar item

→ In the **Calendar** pane, drag the item to a different date or to a different time slot.

→ In the **Calendar** pane, in Day view, Work Week view, or Week view, drag the top or bottom border of an appointment or meeting up or down to change the start or end time.

→ In the **Calendar** pane, click an appointment or meeting one time to select it, press **Ctrl+X**, click the time slot to which you want to move the item, and then press **Ctrl+V**.

→ In the item window, adjust the **Start time** and **End time** settings. Then on the item-specific tab, in the **Actions** group, click **Save & Close**.

To create a copy of an existing appointment

1. In the **Calendar** pane, display the original appointment day and the day to which you want to copy the appointment.

2. Hold down the **Ctrl** key, and drag the appointment to the new date or time slot.

To cancel meetings

1. In the meeting window, on the **Meeting** or **Meeting Series** tab, in the **Actions** group, click **Cancel Meeting**.

2. In the message header, click **Send Cancellation**.

Objective 3.2 practice tasks

The practice file for these tasks is located in the **MOSOutlook2016\Objective3** practice file folder. Before you begin, alert two colleagues that you are going to practice scheduling meetings.

➤ Display tomorrow's date in the Calendar pane and do the following:

❑ Create a half-hour appointment from 11:30 A.M. to 12:00 P.M., with the subject <u>MOS Lunch with Jane</u>. Accept all other default settings.

❑ Without opening the appointment window, change the start time of the appointment to 10:30 A.M and the end time to 11:30 A.M.

❑ Specify the location of the appointment as <u>Fourth Coffee</u>.

❑ Set the appointment options so that other Outlook users know that you will be out of the office from 10:30 A.M. to 11:30 A.M. but can't view any appointment details.

➤ Create the following appointment:

❑ A recurring one-hour appointment on the first Monday of the month at 6:00 P.M. with the subject <u>MOS Book Club</u>.

❑ Set the series to start at the beginning of next month and end after six occurrences.

➤ Create the following event:

❑ A two-day event on Tuesday and Wednesday two weeks from now in Portland, Oregon, with the subject <u>MOS Annual Meeting and Retreat</u>.

❑ Show the time as Out of Office.

❑ Attach the **Outlook_3-2** document to the event.

➤ Create the following meeting request:

❑ Request a half-hour meeting with a colleague, with the subject <u>MOS Status Meeting</u>, at 3:00 P.M. tomorrow.

❑ Enter <u>Test – please accept</u> in the Location box, and send the request to your colleague.

➤ Create the following meeting request:

❑ Schedule a one-hour <u>MOS Budget Meeting</u> with two colleagues at the first available time next week.

❑ Configure the meeting to occur at the same time every month for three months.

Objective 3.3: Organize and manage appointments, meetings, and events

Configure settings for calendar items

As you can with other Outlook items, you can set the importance of a calendar item. Unlike other items, however, the importance is visible only in the open item window. However, you can use the importance setting, as you can any tag, as a way of locating specific calendar items.

By default, Outlook displays a reminder message 15 minutes before the start time of an appointment or meeting, and 18 hours before an all-day event—you can change the reminder to occur as far as two weeks in advance, or you can turn it off completely if you want to.

You might find it necessary to change the date, time, or location of an appointment, meeting, or event. When you are the meeting organizer, you can change any information in a meeting request at any time, including adding or removing invited attendees, or canceling the meeting.

Meeting updates alert attendees to changes and provide response options

After you edit or cancel a meeting, Outlook sends an updated meeting request to the invited attendees to keep them informed. If the only change you make is to the attendee list, Outlook gives you the option of sending an update only to the affected attendees.

To categorize calendar items

→ On the item-specific tab of the item window, in the **Tags** group, click **Categorize**, and then click the category you want to assign.

→ In the **Calendar** pane, select the calendar item. On the item-specific tool tab, in the **Tags** group, click **Categorize**, and then click the category you want to assign.

→ In the **Calendar** pane, right-click the calendar item, click **Categorize**, and then click the category you want to assign.

To set calendar item importance

→ On the item-specific tab of the item window, in the **Tags** group, click the **High Importance** button or **Low Importance** button.

→ In the **Calendar** pane, select the item. On the item-specific tool tab, in the **Tags** group, click the **High Importance** button or **Low Importance** button.

Tip If you set the importance of a single occurrence of a recurring item, the High Importance and Low Importance buttons are unavailable in the Calendar pane.

To configure reminders

→ On the item-specific tab of the item window, in the **Options** group, in the **Reminder** list, click the amount of time prior to the item start time that you want the reminder time to appear.

→ In the **Calendar** pane, select the item. On the item-specific tool tab, in the **Options** group, in the **Reminder** list, click the amount of time prior to the item start time that you want the reminder time to appear.

To update calendar items

1. Double-click the item on your calendar.

2. If the item is one of a series (a recurring item), click to indicate whether you want to edit the series or only the selected instance.

3. Make the changes you want, and then save the item.

4. If the item is a meeting, send the meeting update to the attendees.

Manage meeting options

When you receive a meeting request from another Outlook user, the meeting appears on your calendar with your time scheduled as Tentative. Until you respond to the meeting request, the organizer doesn't know whether you plan to attend.

Meetings are marked as Tentative and details are dimmed until you accept the request

By default, meeting requests that you send include a standard set of response options. You can respond to a meeting request in one of these four ways:

- Accept the request. Outlook deletes the meeting request and adds the meeting to your calendar.

- Tentatively accept the request, which indicates that you might be able to attend the meeting but are undecided. Outlook deletes the meeting request and shows the meeting on your calendar as tentatively scheduled.

- Propose a new meeting time. Outlook sends your request to the meeting organizer for confirmation and shows the meeting with the original time on your calendar as tentatively scheduled.

- Decline the request. Outlook deletes the meeting request and removes the meeting from your calendar.

In addition to these, you have the option to reply to the meeting organizer or to all attendees, or to forward the meeting request. When you forward a meeting request for which you are not the organizer, the meeting request is sent from you "on behalf of" the meeting organizer, and responses are sent to the meeting organizer.

If you don't respond to a meeting request, the meeting remains on your calendar with your time shown as tentatively scheduled and the meeting details in gray font rather than black.

	MONDAY	TUESDAY	WEDNESDAY	THURSDAY	FRIDAY
	7	8	9	10	11
				Pay Day	
8 AM					
9	Sales team meeting	MOS wrap-up: Skype Mee		Working from home	
10		Spring product launch promotion Tailspin Toys Joan Lambert			
11					
12 PM					Conf call with Tailspin
1					
2			Staff meeting Conference Room 1 Joan Lambert		

Accepted and unaccepted meetings in Work Week view

If you're unsure whether a meeting time works for you, you can click the 'Calendar Preview link in the meeting request to display your calendar for the time period immediately surrounding the meeting, or you can click the Calendar button at the top of the meeting request to open your default calendar for the suggested meeting day in a separate window. If the meeting time doesn't work for you, you can propose a new time.

You can propose a new meeting time to the meeting organizer

When accepting or declining a meeting, you can choose whether to send a response to the meeting organizer. If you don't send a response, your acceptance will not be tallied, and the organizer will not know whether you are planning to attend the meeting. If you do send a response, you can add a message to the meeting organizer before sending it.

If you are the meeting organizer, you can add an attendee to a meeting at any time. If this is the only change you make to the attendee list, Outlook gives you the option of sending an update only to the new attendee.

You can take notes for any meeting in Microsoft OneNote. If you originate the notes from within the meeting request, the notes are linked to the meeting request and include all the information from the meeting request, in addition to a link back to it. If you store the notes in a shared OneNote notebook, you can make the notes available to other meeting attendees.

To respond to meeting invitations

1. In the meeting window, in the **Reading Pane**, or on the shortcut menu that appears when you right-click the meeting request, click **Accept**, **Tentative**, or **Decline**.

2. Choose whether to send a standard response, a personalized response, or no response at all.

To propose a new time for a meeting

1. In the meeting window or in the **Reading Pane**, click **Propose New Time**, and then click **Tentative and Propose New Time** or **Decline and Propose New Time** to open the Propose New Time dialog box.

2. In the **Propose New Time** dialog box, change the meeting start and end times to the times you want to propose, either by dragging the start time and end time bars or by changing the date and time in the lists, and then click **Propose Time**.

3. In the meeting response window that opens, enter a message to the meeting organizer if you want to, and then click **Send** to send your response and add the meeting to your calendar as tentatively scheduled for the original meeting time. If the meeting organizer approves the meeting time change, you and other attendees will receive updated meeting requests showing the new meeting time.

To forward meeting requests

1. In the meeting window, on the **Meeting** or **Meeting Series** tab, in the **Respond** group, click **Respond**, and then click **Forward**.

2. Enter the recipient's email address and send the meeting request.

3

To add meeting participants

1. Display the meeting window and enter new attendees by using any of the previously described methods.

2. To the left of the **To** box, click **Send Update**.

3. In the **Send Update to Attendees** dialog box, click **Send updates only to added or deleted attendees**, and then click **OK**.

To share meeting notes

1. In the meeting window, on the **Meeting** or **Meeting Series** tab, in the **Meeting Notes** group, click **Meeting Notes**.

2. In the **Meeting Notes** window, click **Share notes with the meeting** or **Take notes on your own**.

3. In the **Choose Notes to Share with Meeting or Select Location in OneNote** dialog box, select the OneNote location in which you want to store the meeting notes, and then click **OK**.

4. Record your meeting notes in the OneNote window that opens.

Objective 3.3 practice tasks

Use the *MOS Budget Meeting* and *MOS Status Meeting* calendar items that you created in the Objective 3.2 practice tasks as practice files for these tasks. Before you begin, alert your two colleagues that you are going to practice updating and canceling meetings.

➤ Do the following for the *MOS Lunch with Jane* appointment:

❑ Set a reminder to appear at 9:30 A.M. on the day of the appointment.

➤ Do the following for the *MOS Budget Meeting*:

❑ Reschedule the meeting to the week after next.

❑ Indicate that the meeting is high priority.

❑ Send the updated meeting request.

➤ Ask a colleague to send you a meeting request for a meeting with the subject *MOS Project Meeting*. When the meeting request arrives, do the following:

❑ Tentatively accept the meeting and propose that the meeting be held at the same time on the following day.

❑ Forward the meeting from your calendar to your other colleague.

❑ From the meeting window, create a shared notes page for the meeting in OneNote.

➤ Do the following for the *MOS Status Meeting*:

❑ Add a second colleague as an optional attendee.

❑ Send the updated meeting request to only the new attendee.

➤ Cancel the *MOS Budget Meeting* meetings and send cancellation notices to the attendees.

Objective 3.4:
Create and manage notes and tasks

Create tasks

If you use your Outlook task list to its fullest potential, you'll frequently add tasks to it. You can create tasks in several ways:

- In the Tasks module, add a task to the task list.
- In other modules, add a task to the Tasks peek.
- Create a new task in the task window.
- Base a task on an existing Outlook item (such as a message).

Just as you can create recurring appointments, events, and meetings, you can create recurring tasks. You can set the task to occur every day, week, month, or year; or you can specify that a new task should be generated a certain amount of time after the last task is complete.

A typical task

Regardless of how or where you create a task, all tasks are available in the Tasks module and in the Tasks peek. Only individual tasks are available in the Tasks List.

You will frequently need to take action based on information you receive in Outlook—for example, information in a message or meeting request. You can add information from another Outlook item to your task list, to ensure that you complete any necessary follow-up work. Depending on the method you use, you can either create a new task from an existing item or simply transfer the existing item to your task list by flagging it.

Tip When viewing your calendar in Day, Work Week, or Week view, each item on your Outlook task list appears in the Tasks section below its due date. You can schedule specific time to complete a task by dragging it from the Tasks area to your calendar.

To create a task in the Tasks module

→ On the **Home** tab, in the **New** group, click **New Task**. Enter the task details in the task window that opens, and then save and close the task.

→ When displaying the To-Do List view of the Tasks module, enter the task description in the **Type a new task** box, and then press **Enter** to create a task with the default settings.

→ When displaying the Tasks List view of the Tasks module, enter the task description in the **Click here to add a new Task** box, press **Tab** to move to subsequent fields, fill in other information, and then press **Enter**.

To create a task in any module

→ On the **Home** tab, in the **New** group, in the **New Items** list, click **Task**.

→ Press **Ctrl+Shift+K**.

→ In the **Tasks** peek, enter the task description in the **Type a new task** box.

To create a task from an email message, contact record, or note

→ Drag the message, contact record, or note to the **Tasks** button on the **Navigation Bar**.

Tip The task window that opens contains the information from the original item.

To transfer an email message to your task list without creating an individual task

→ In the **Mail** pane, click the flag icon to the right of a message.

This method, referred to as *flagging a message for follow-up*, adds the message to your task lists with the default due date specified in the Quick Click settings, and adds an information bar to the message. However, it does not create a separate task item, so to retain the task, you must retain the message—you can move the message between mail folders, but deleting the message also deletes the task.

→ In the **Mail** pane, right-click the flag icon to the right of a message, and then specify a due date: **Today**, **Tomorrow**, **This Week**, **Next Week**, **No Date**, or **Custom** (which allows you to set specific start and end dates).

→ Drag the message to the **Tasks** peek and drop it under the heading for the due date you want to assign it to. (If the desired due date doesn't already have a heading in the **Tasks** peek, drop the message under another heading and then assign the due date you want.)

This method also adds the message to your task list but doesn't create a separate task item.

Manage tasks

To help you organize your tasks, you can assign them to color categories in the same way that you do any other Outlook item.

When you create a task item, the only information you must include is the subject. As with many other types of Outlook items, you can set several options for tasks to make it easier to organize and identify tasks.

- **Start date and due date** You can display tasks on either the start date or the due date in the various Outlook task lists. The color of the task flag indicates the due date.

- **Status** You can track the status of a task to remind yourself of your progress. Specific status options include Not Started, In Progress, Completed, Waiting On Someone Else, or Deferred. You also have the option of indicating what percentage of the task is complete. Setting the percentage complete to 25%, 50%, or 75% sets the task status to In Progress. Setting it to 100% sets the task status to Complete.

- **Priority** Unless you indicate otherwise, a task is created with a Normal priority level. You can set the priority to add a visual indicator of a task's importance. The Low Importance setting displays a blue downward-pointing arrow, and the High Importance setting displays a red exclamation point. You can sort and filter tasks based on their priority.

- **Recurrence** You can set a task to recur on a regular basis; for example, you might create a Payroll task that recurs every month. Only the current instance of a recurring task appears in your task list. When you mark the current task as complete, Outlook creates the next instance of the task.

- **Category** Tasks use the same category list as other Outlook items. You can assign a task to a category to associate it with related items such as messages and appointments.

- **Reminder** You can set a reminder for a task in the same way you do for an appointment. The reminder appears until you dismiss it or mark the task as complete.

- **Privacy** Marking a task as private ensures that other Outlook users to whom you delegate account access can't see the task details.

None of the options are required, but they can be helpful when sorting, filtering, and prioritizing your tasks.

To track tasks to completion, you can update the Status and % Complete settings in the task window.

Tip You can attach files to tasks, and you can include text, tables, charts, illustrations, hyperlinks, and other content in the task window content pane.

You can remove a task from your active task list by marking it as complete, or by deleting it. You can remove a flagged item from the active task list by removing the follow-up flag.

🗋 ✅	SUBJECT	DUE DATE ▲	CATEGORIES	☇
	Click here to add a new Task			
✅	~~company taxes~~	~~Fri 4/1/2016~~	☐	✓
✅	~~Get Trinity's phone working~~	~~Fri 4/1/2016~~	▨ Personal	✓
✅	~~Invoice clients (1st 15th)~~	~~Sun 10/16/2016~~	▪ OTSI	✓
✅	~~16794 mortgage w/d from bank~~	~~Tue 11/1/2016~~	▪ Financial	✓
✅	~~Invoice clients (16th eom)~~	~~Tue 11/1/2016~~	▪ OTSI	✓
☐	Reserve team dinner venue	Mon 11/7/2016	☐	▷
☐	Send Management Dinner invitations	Wed 11/9/2016	☐	▷
☐	Update OTSI D&B listing	Fri 11/11/2016	☐	▷
☐	Order new brochures	Sat 11/12/2016	☐	▷
☐	Invoice clients (1st-15th)	Wed 11/16/2016	▪ OTSI	▷
☐	16794 mortgage w/d from bank	Thu 12/1/2016	▪ Financial	▷
☐	Invoice clients (16th-eom)	Thu 12/1/2016	▪ OTSI	▷

Active and completed tasks

After you mark an instance of a recurring task as complete, Outlook generates a new instance of the task at whatever interval you specified when creating the task.

Removing the flag from a flagged item such as a message or contact record retains the item in its original location but removes it from your task list entirely.

To create a recurring task

1. On the **Task** tab of the task window, in the **Recurrence** group, click **Recurrence**.

2. In the **Task Recurrence** dialog box, select the **Recurrence pattern** and **Range of recurrence** options you want, and then click **OK**.

To assign a task to a category

→ In your **To-Do List** or **Tasks** peek, right-click the category icon to the right of the task subject in the task list, click **Categorize**, and then click the category you want.

→ Click the task in your **Tasks List** to select it. On the **Home** tab, in the **Tags** group, click **Categorize**, and then click the category you want.

→ On the **Task** tab of the task window, in the **Tags** group, click **Categorize**, and then click the category you want.

To assign a due date to a task

→ In your **To-Do List** or **Tasks** peek, right-click the flag icon, and then click the due date you want.

To mark a task as private

→ On the **Task** tab of the task window, in the **Tags** group, click the **Private** button.

To mark a task as complete

→ In the task window, set **% Complete** to **100%**.

→ On the **Task** tab of the task window, in the **Manage Task** group, click **Mark Complete**.

To delete a task

→ In your **To-Do List** or **Tasks** peek, right-click the task subject, and then click **Delete**.

→ On the **Task** tab of the task window, in the **Actions** group, click **Delete**.

→ In the Tasks module, in the **To-Do List** or **Tasks List**, click the flagged item to select it. Then on the **Home** tab, in the **Delete** group, click **Delete**.

To remove a follow-up flag

→ Display the Tasks module, click the flagged item to select it, and then click **Remove from List** in the **Manage Task** group on the **Home** tab.

→ Click the flagged item in the **Tasks** peek, and then click **Remove from List** in the **Manage Task** group on the **Task List** tool tab.

→ Right-click the flagged item, click **Follow Up**, and then click **Clear Flag**.

Create and manage notes

In the Notes module, you can create and store text notes about any subject. If your organization uses Exchange Server, the notes are available to you whenever you connect to your account through Outlook, through your Internet browser, or from a mobile device.

Tip Outlook Notes support plain text, formatted text, and hyperlinks. You can't format text within a note but you can paste formatted text from a document, message, or other source into a note and retain its formatting.

Some functionality of the Notes feature in Outlook 2016 has been modified from that of previous versions, as follows:

- The Notes folder is still available in the Folder List, and the Notes module is available from the Navigation Bar.

- Notes options are not available in the Outlook Options dialog box. You can create new notes, but only with the default color and font settings. (The note color does change to reflect any color categories that you assign to it.)

- Linking from a note to a contact record is no longer possible; however, you can attach a note to a contact record from within the contact record.

Storing information in the Notes module

You can view the content of the Notes module in three standard views:

- **Icon view** This view depicts each note as a colored square with a turned up corner, reminiscent of a pad of sticky notes.

  In Icon view, you can display large icons organized in rows and columns, or small icons organized either in rows or in columns.

- **Notes List view** This list view displays a small icon, the note subject, and up to three lines of note content.

- **Last 7 Days view** This view is identical to Notes List view but displays only notes that have been modified within the last seven days.

In either list view, you can choose from two standard arrangements: Categories and Created Date. As with other list views, you can sort notes by a specific field by clicking the column header for that field, and you can add or remove fields from the list view.

Tip The first line of text in the note is shown as its subject.

You can organize notes by assigning them to color categories. In Icon view, uncategorized notes are depicted in the default color set in the Outlook Options window; categorized notes are depicted in the most recently assigned category color. You can also attach notes to other Outlook items, such as contact records.

To create notes

- → In the Notes module, do either of the following:
  - On the **Home** tab, in the **New** group, click **New Note**.
  - Press **Ctrl+N**.
- → In any module, press **Ctrl+Shift+N**.

Tip In Outlook 2016, Notes are not included on the New Items menu of other modules.

To assign one or more notes to a color category

1. In the **Notes** pane, select the note or notes you want to assign to the same category.

2. On the **Home** tab, in the **Tags** group, click **Categorize** and then, in the list, click the category you want to assign.

To attach a note to a contact record

1. Open the contact record window.

2. On the **Insert** tab, in the **Include** group, click **Outlook Item**.

3. In the **Insert Item** dialog box, in the **Look in** list, click the **Notes** folder, and then, in the **Items** list, click the note you want to attach.

4. In the **Insert as** area, do one of the following:

   - To insert the note content in the **Notes** pane of the contact record, click **Text only**.

   - To attach the note in the **Notes** pane of the contact record, click **Attachment**.

   - To create a link to the note in the **Notes** pane of the contact record, click **Shortcut**.

5. In the **Insert Item** dialog box, click **OK**.

Objective 3.4 practice tasks

There are no practice files for these tasks.

➤ From the To-Do Bar, do the following:

❑ Create a task with the subject <u>MOS Dinner Reservations</u>.

❑ Flag the task for completion this week.

❑ Assign the task to the Management category (or another category you choose).

➤ Open a new task window, and do the following:

❑ Create a task with the subject <u>MOS Send Dinner Invitations</u>.

❑ Set a due date of next Tuesday with a reminder at 5:00 P.M.

❑ Set the status to Waiting On Someone Else.

➤ Open the MOS Dinner Reservations task and do the following:

❑ Mark the task as private and high priority.

❑ Set the task to 25 percent complete.

➤ Create a new task with the subject <u>MOS Status Report</u> that must be completed on the first Monday of every month for six months.

➤ In the Notes module, do the following:

❑ Create a note that contains your full name.

❑ Modify the note content so that only your first name appears as the note subject, and your last name is in the note body.

❑ If you haven't already done so, create a color category named <u>MOS</u>. Assign the note to the MOS color category.

Objective group 4

Manage contacts and groups

The skills tested in this section of the Microsoft Office Specialist exam for Microsoft Outlook 2016 relate to the storage and management of information about people. Specifically, the following objectives are associated with this set of skills:

4.1 Create and manage contacts

4.2 Create and manage contact groups

Having immediate access to current, accurate contact information for the people you need to interact with—by email, phone, mail, or otherwise—is important for timely and effective communication.

You can easily build and maintain a detailed contact list, or address book, in the Outlook People module. Within each address book, you can create contact records for individuals or companies that store various types of information about people you correspond with, such as business associates, customers, suppliers, family members, and friends. From your address book, you can look up information, create email messages, and schedule meetings. You can share stored contact information with other people.

To simplify communication with multiple contacts. Contact groups can consist of existing and new contacts, and can also store notes about the group.

This chapter guides you in studying ways of storing contact information for people and for groups of people you want to communicate with by email or other electronic means.

4

To complete the practice tasks in this chapter, you need the practice file contained in the **MOSOutlook2016\Objective4** practice file folder. For more information, see "Download the practice files" in this book's introduction.

Objective 4.1: Create and manage contacts

Create and modify contact records

You save contact information for people and companies by creating a contact record in an address book.

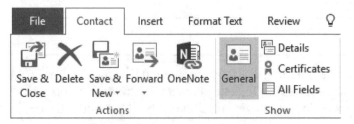

A contact record that includes business contact information and a photo

A contact record has multiple pages. Most of the information is stored on the General page. You change pages by clicking the buttons in the Show group on the Contact tab.

Almost all work with contact records is on the General page

On the General page of a contact record, you can store the following types of contact information:

- Name, company name, and job title
- Business, home, and alternate addresses
- Business, home, mobile, pager, and other phone numbers
- Business, home, and alternate fax numbers
- Webpage address (URL), instant messaging (IM) address, and up to three email addresses

> **Tip** If you need to store more than three email addresses for a contact, you can do so by creating a custom contact record form.

- An identifying image such as a photo or company logo
- General notes, which can include text and illustrations such as photos, clip art images, SmartArt diagrams, charts, and shapes

On the Details page of a contact record, you can store personal and organization-specific details, such as the following:

- Professional information, including department, office location, profession, manager's name, and assistant's name
- Personal information, including nickname, spouse or partner's name, birthday, anniversary, and the title (such as Miss, Mrs., or Ms.) and suffix (such as Jr. or Sr.) for use in correspondence

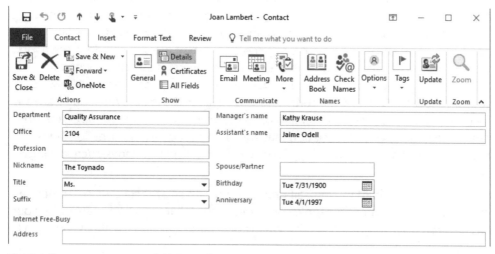

The Details page stores some useful information

You typically create a contact record by displaying the address book to which you want to add the contact record in the People module and then clicking the New Contact button in the New group on the Home tab. In the contact record window that opens, you insert the information you want to save. After you save the contact record, it appears in the contact list.

You can create a contact record that contains only one piece of information (for example, a person's name or a company name), or as much information as you want to include. You can quickly create contact records for several people who work for the same company by cloning the company information from an existing record to a new one. And, of course, you can add to or change the information stored in a contact record at any time.

The order in which Outlook displays contact records in the contact list is controlled by the File As setting. By default, Outlook files contacts by last name (Last, First order). If you prefer, you can change the order for new contacts to any of the following:

- First Last
- Company
- Last, First (Company)
- Company (Last, First)

See Also In addition to creating individual contact records, you can create groups of contacts so that you can message multiple people through one email address. For information, see "Objective 4.2: Create and manage contact groups."

Within each contact record window, information appears not only in the fields of the contact record but also in the form of a graphic that resembles a business card. When you enter a person's contact information in a contact record, basic information appears in the business card shown in the upper-right corner of the contact window. This data includes the person's name, company, and job title; work, mobile, and home phone numbers; and email, postal, webpage, and instant messaging addresses. (Only the first 10 lines of information fit on the card.) If an image is associated with the person through Microsoft Exchange Server, SharePoint, or a social network to which you've connected Outlook, the contact record includes the image. An image from a social network is identified by a small icon in the lower-right corner of the image. You can change the types of information that appear, rearrange the information fields, format the text and background, and add, change, or remove images, such as a logo or photograph.

Creating a business card for yourself provides you with an attractive way of presenting your contact information to people you correspond with in email. You can attach your business card to an outgoing email message or include it as part (or all) of your email signature. The recipient of your business card can easily create a contact record for you by saving the business card to his or her Outlook address book.

See Also For information about email signatures, see "Objective 2.1: Configure mail settings."

To create a new contact record

1. Open a new contact record window by doing any of the following:

   - In the People module, on the **Home** tab, in the **New** group, click the **New Contact** button.

   - In any module, on the **Home** tab, in the **New** group, click the **New Items** button, and then click **Contact**.

   - In any module, press **Ctrl+Shift+C**.

2. Enter at least one piece of identifying information for the contact.

3. On the **Contact** tab, in the **Actions** group, click the **Save & Close** button.

To create a contact record based on an existing contact record

1. Open the existing (source) contact record window.

2. On the **Contact** tab, in the **Actions** group, click the **Save & New** arrow, and then click **Contact from the Same Company**.

Tip Double-clicking a contact in People view displays the contact information in a People card rather than in a contact record window. You cannot create a duplicate contact record from a People card. Double-clicking a contact in any view other than People view displays the contact information in a contact record window.

To create a contact record for a message sender or recipient

→ In the **Reading Pane** or in the message reading window, right-click the message sender or recipient in the message header, and then click **Add to Outlook Contacts**.

To edit a contact record

→ To edit a contact record from the People module, do either of the following:

   - In People view, display the contact record in the **Reading Pane**, and then in the upper-right corner of the contract record, click the **Edit** link.

   - In any view of the People module, double-click the contact.

→ To edit a contact record from the Mail module, in the **Reading Pane**, right-click the message sender or recipient in the message header, and then click **Edit Contact**.

→ To edit a contact record from a message reading window, right-click the message sender or recipient in the message header, and then click **Edit Contact**.

4

To add an image to a contact record

1. In the contact record window, on the **Contact** tab, in the **Options** group, click **Picture**, and then click **Add Picture**.

2. In the **Add Contact Picture** window, browse to and select the picture you want to attach to the contact record, and then click **Open**.

To change a contact record image

1. In the contact record window, on the **Contact** tab, in the **Options** group, click **Picture**, and then click **Change Picture**.

2. In the **Change Contact Picture** window, browse to and select the picture you want to attach to the contact record, and then click **Open**.

To remove a contact record image

→ In the contact record window, on the **Contact** tab, in the **Options** group, click **Picture**, and then click **Remove Picture**.

To assign a contact record to a category

→ Select the contact record. On the **Home** tab, in the **Tags** group, click **Categorize**, and then click the category you want to assign.

To set the filing order for all contact records

1. Open the **Outlook Options** dialog box and display the **People** page.

2. In the **Names and filing** section, click the **Default "File As" Order** arrow and then, in the list, click the order you want.

3. In the **Outlook Options** dialog box, click **OK** to save the changes.

To set the filing order for an individual contact record

→ In the contact record window, expand the **File as** list, and then click *First Last*; *Company*; *Last, First* (*Company*); or *Company* (*Last, First*).

To delete a contact record

→ In the People module, select the contact record, and then do any of the following:

- Press the **Delete** key.
- On the **Home** tab, in the **Delete** group, click the **Delete** button.
- Press **Ctrl+D**.

Store contact records

Contact records are stored in address books. When you configure Outlook to connect to an email account, you automatically have a default address book, which Outlook displays when you click the People button on the Navigation Bar. The default address book content is stored in a folder named *Contacts*. If you connect to an Exchange Server account, the default address book is part of that account, and the information you store in the address book is available on all computers and devices from which you connect to your account.

You display and work with address books in the People module. The content pane of the People module displays the contact records saved in the currently selected address book. The default view of contact records in Outlook 2016 is a new format named People cards, but you can choose from several standard views, including business cards, text-only cards, and various lists.

People cards display selected contact information compiled from the contact records you store in Outlook and any social networks you connect to.

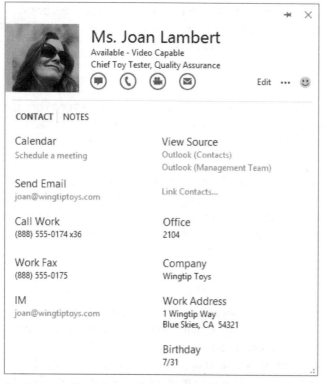

People cards collate information from multiple sources

Contacts address books

Outlook creates a Contacts address book for each account and social network you connect to. These address books are available from the My Contacts list in the Folder Pane of the People module.

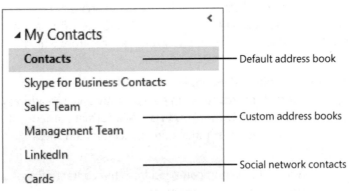

Address books can come from many sources

The Contacts address book of your default email account is your main address book, and it is the address book that appears by default in the People module. The Contacts address book is empty until you add contact records to it.

Custom address books

You can create additional address books; for example, you might want to keep contact information for family and friends in an address book separate from client contact information, or you might maintain an address book for clients that meet specific criteria.

When you display the Folder List in the Folder Pane, your custom address books appear along with other folders you create, and you can organize them in the same manner—for example, at the same level as your Inbox, as a subfolder of the Contacts address book, or inside a project folder. All address books are available from the My Contacts list in the Folder Pane of the People module.

Global Address Lists

If you have an Exchange account, you also have access to an official address book called the Global Address List (or *GAL*). The GAL is maintained by your organization's Exchange administrator and includes information about individuals within your organization, distribution lists, and resources (such as conference rooms and media equipment) that you can reserve when you schedule meetings. It can also include organizational information (each person's manager and direct subordinates) and group membership information (the distribution lists each person belongs to).

The GAL doesn't appear in the My Contacts list shown in the Folder Pane of the People module. Outlook users can view the GAL but not change its contents. Only an Exchange administrator can modify the GAL.

To create a custom address book

1. Display the **Folder** tab of any module.

2. In the **New** group, click the **New Folder** button (or press **Ctrl+Shift+E**).

3. In the **Create New Folder** dialog box, do the following, and then click **OK**:

   a. In the **Name** box, enter a descriptive name for the address book.

   b. In the **Folder contains** list, click **Contact Items**.

   c. In the **Select where to place the folder** box, click your primary address book, if you want to store all address books in one directory structure, or any other location in which you want to store the new address book.

To display an address book in the People module

➜ In the **My Contacts** list, click the address book you want to display.

Share contact records and address books

You can send individual contact records to other people in an Outlook-specific format or as a vCard file (a virtual business card). You can send a contact group only in the Outlook-specific format, so the recipient must be another Outlook user.

If you want to share the contents of a custom address book with other people, you can do so by sending a sharing invitation. If the other people are within your Exchange organization, you have the option of allowing the other users to update the contact records in the address book.

Another way to share contact information is by importing contact records from external files or locations, and exporting contact records to send to other people.

You can import data into Outlook from data files created in Outlook (.pst files) or from plain-text files that contain field values separated by commas (.csv files). Similarly, you can export contact records from Outlook in those same formats so that other people can import them into Outlook or another program.

> **See Also** For information about exporting Outlook items, see "Objective 1.2: Print and save information."

To send a contact record or contact group record by email

➜ Right-click the contact or contact group, click **Forward Contact**, and then click **As a Business Card** or **As an Outlook Contact**.

4

To share an address book

1. Do either of the following:
   - In the **My Contacts** list, right-click the address book, click **Share**, and then click **Share Contacts**.
   - Display the address book. On the **Folder** tab, in the **Share** group, click the **Share Contacts** button.

You can stipulate whether the recipient can edit shared contact records

2. In the **Sharing invitation** message window that opens, do the following, and then click **Send**:

   a. In the **To** box, enter the email addresses of the people with whom you want to share the address book.

   b. If you want to allow other people to modify the address book content, select the **Recipient can add, edit, and delete items in this contacts folder** check box.

To import contact records from a comma-separated values file or an Outlook data file

1. On the **Open & Export** page of the Backstage view, click **Import/Export** to start the Import And Export Wizard and display a list of actions that you can perform by using the wizard.

2. In the **Choose an action to perform** list, click **Import from another program or file**, and then click **Next** to display the list of file types from which you can import content.

3. In the **Select file type to import from** list, click **Comma Separated Values** or **Outlook Data File (.pst)**, and then click **Next**.

4. Click the **Browse** button to the right of the **File to import** box to open the Browse dialog box. In the **Browse** dialog box, navigate to the file you want to import, and then click **OK**.

5. In the **Options** area, click one of these options for handling contact records that match existing contact records in the address book into which you import them:

   - **Replace duplicates with items imported**
   - **Allow duplicates to be created**
   - **Do not import duplicate items**

6. Click **Next** to display a list of the folders in your Outlook installation.

7. In the **Select destination folder** list, click the address book into which you want to import the contact records, and then click **Next**.

8. If the fields defined in the file you're importing do not use the same field names as an Outlook contact record, click the **Map Custom Fields** button. Then in the **Map Custom Fields** dialog box, match named fields from the source file to Outlook field names. When you finish, click **OK**.

9. On the last page of the **Import a File Wizard**, click **Finish** to import the contact records into the selected address book.

To import contact records from a source file type other than .csv or .pst

→ Export the contact records from the source file to a .csv file, and then import the .csv file.

To import contact records into a separate address book

→ First create the address book. Then import the contact records and specify the address book as the import location.

◇◇

Exam Strategy You can import a SharePoint contact list as an address book. Doing so is beyond the scope of Exam 77-731. "Outlook 2016: Core Communication, Collaboration and Email Skills."

◇◇

4

Objective 4.1 practice tasks

The practice file for these tasks is located in the **MOSOutlook2016\Objective4** practice file folder.

➤ Create a new contact record.

    ❏ Enter the following information:

Full name	<u>John Evans</u>
Company	<u>Wingtip Toys</u>
Job title	<u>Assembly Plant Manager</u>
Email	<u>john@wingtiptoys.com</u>
Webpage address	<u>www.wingtiptoys.com</u>
Business address	<u>315 Wingtip Way</u> <u>Highflying, TX 71234</u>

    ❏ Add the **Outlook_4-1** image to the contact record.

    ❏ Save the contact record.

➤ Create a contact record based on the *John Evans* contact record.

    ❏ Add the following information to the base contact record:

Full name	<u>Heidi Steen</u>
Job title	<u>Sales Associate</u>
Email	<u>heidi@wingtiptoys.com</u>

➤ Edit the John Evans contact record as follows:

    ❏ Change the filing order from *Evans, John* to *John Evans*.

    ❏ Note that John's nickname is <u>Jack</u>, his spouse's name is <u>Jill</u>, and his birthday is <u>January 1, 1987</u>.

➤ If you haven't already done so, create a contact record for yourself and do the following:

    ❏ Include your name, company, job title, one or more phone numbers, one or more email addresses, and one or more postal addresses.

    ❏ Forward your contact record to a friend as a vCard.

    ❏ Enter <u>MOS Contact Information</u> as the message subject, embed your business card as a signature, and send the message.

➤ Create an address book as follows:

❑ Name the address book <u>MOS Contacts</u>.

❑ Store the address book in your default Contacts folder.

❑ Move the *John Evans* and *Heidi Steen* contact records to the new address book.

➤ Share the *MOS Contacts* address book with a friend. Configure the sharing settings so that the recipient can display, but not change, the contact records in the shared address book.

Objective 4.2:
Create and manage contact groups

If you frequently send messages to specific groups of people, such as members of a project team, club, or family, you can create a contact group that contains all the email addresses. Then you can send a message to all the group members by addressing it to the contact group.

Contact groups are like personal versions of distribution lists. A distribution list is available to everyone on your Exchange Server network; a contact group is available only from the local address book you store it in. You can, however, distribute a contact group to other people for their own use.

The ribbon provides a separate tab of commands for managing contact groups.

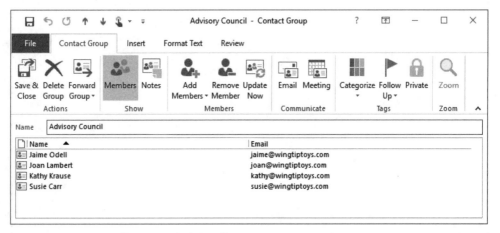

Contact groups are stored in your Outlook data file

You add a member to a contact group either by selecting an existing contact record from an address book or by entering contact information in the Add New Member dialog box. When you add a member by using the latter method, you have the option to simultaneously create a contact record for him or her.

When you send a message to a contact group, each member of the contact group receives a copy of the message. If you want to send a message to most, but not all, members of a contact group, you can expand the contact group in the address field to a full list of its members, and remove individual people for the specific message at the time you send it.

To create a contact group

1. Open a new contact group record window by doing any of the following:

   - In the People module, on the **Home** tab, in the **New** group, click the **New Contact Group** button.

   - In any module, on the **Home** tab, in the **New** group, click the **New Items** button, click **More Items**, and then click **Contact Group**.

     > IMPORTANT If you have an Exchange account, *Group* appears on the New Items menu. This command creates an Exchange-specific group, not a local contact group.

   - In any module, press **Ctrl+Shift+L**.

2. In the **Name** box, enter a name for the contact group.

3. On the **Contact Group** tab, in the **Actions** group, click the **Save & Close** button.

To open a contact group for editing

→ In the **People Pane**, double-click the contact group to open it in a contact group window.

To add members to an open contact group

1. On the **Contact Group** tab, in the **Members** group, click the **Add Members** button, and then click **From Address Book**.

2. In the **Select Members** dialog box, in the **Address Book** list, click the address book from which you want to add one or more contacts.

3. In the **Name** list, double-click the name of each contact you want to add.

4. In the **Select Members** dialog box, click **OK**.

Or

1. On the **Contact Group** tab, in the **Members** group, click the **Add Members** button, and then click **New Email Contact**.

   > Tip Outlook user interface elements refer to electronic mail as *email* or *e-mail*. For consistency, the text of this book always references electronic mail as *email*.

2. In the **Add New Member** dialog box, enter information in the **Display name** and **Email address** fields.

3. If you want Outlook to also create a contact record for this person, select the **Add to Contacts** check box.

4. In the **Add New Member** dialog box, click **OK**.

4

To remove members from a contact group

1. Open the contact group window.

2. In the contact group member list, click the contact you want to remove.

Tip You can select multiple contacts for simultaneous removal by holding down the Ctrl key and clicking each contact.

---

3. On the **Contact Group** tab, in the **Members** group, click the **Remove Member** button.

4. Save and close the contact group.

To update a member's information within a contact group

1. Open the contact group window.

2. On the **Contact Group** tab, in the **Members** group, click the **Update Now** button.

3. Save and close the contact group.

To add notes to a contact group

1. In the contact group window, in the **Show** group, click the **Notes** button.

2. On the **Notes** page, enter notes in the form of text, images, and other content.

To delete a contact group

→   In the address book, select the contact group, and then do any of the following:

- Press the **Delete** key.
- On the **Home** tab, in the **Delete** group, click the **Delete** button.
- Press **Ctrl+D**.

Objective 4.2 practice tasks

Use the *MOS Contacts* address book you created in the Objective 4.1 practice tasks to complete these tasks.

➤ In the *MOS Contacts* address book, do the following:

❑ Create a new contact group named <u>MOS Clients</u>.

❑ Select the John Evans contact record you created earlier in this chapter as a member.

❑ Add Heidi Steen to the contact group.

❑ Save and close the contact group.

➤ Open the *MOS Clients* contact group and do the following:

❑ Add the following people to the contact group and to your contact list:

<u>Holly Dickson</u>	<u>holly@consolidatedmessenger.com</u>
<u>Max Stevens</u>	<u>max@consolidatedmessenger.com</u>
<u>Linda Mitchell</u>	<u>linda@lucernepublishing.com</u>
<u>Jill Shrader</u>	<u>jill@lucernepublishing.com</u>

❑ Save and close the contact group.

➤ Open the contact record for Jill Shrader and do the following:

❑ Change her email address to <u>jill@wingtiptoys.com</u>.

❑ Save and close the contact record.

➤ Open the *MOS Clients* contact group and do the following:

❑ Update the contact group to reflect Jill Shrader's new email address.

❑ Remove Holly Dickson from the contact group.

❑ Add a note to the contact group that says <u>Created while practicing for the MOS Outlook 2016 exam.</u>

❑ Save and close the contact group.

➤ Send a message to the <u>MOS Clients</u> contact group with the subject <u>MOS Group Test</u>. (You will receive nondeliverable message alerts in response.)

Index

About the author

 **JOAN LAMBERT** has worked closely with Microsoft technologies since 1986, and in the training and certification industry since 1997. As President and CEO of Online Training Solutions, Inc. (OTSI), Joan guides the translation of technical information and requirements into useful, relevant, and measurable resources for people who are seeking certification of their computer skills or who simply want to know how to get things done efficiently.

Joan is the author or coauthor of more than four dozen books about Windows and Office (for Windows, Mac, and iPad), five generations of Microsoft Office Specialist certification study guides, video-based training courses for SharePoint and OneNote, QuickStudy guides for Windows and Office, and the GO! series book for Outlook 2016.

Blissfully based in America's Finest City, Joan is a Microsoft Certified Professional, Microsoft Office Specialist Master (for all versions of Office since Office 2003), Microsoft Certified Technology Specialist (for Windows and Windows Server), Microsoft Certified Technology Associate (for Windows), Microsoft Dynamics Specialist, and Microsoft Certified Trainer.

ONLINE TRAINING SOLUTIONS, INC. (OTSI) specializes in the design and creation of Microsoft Office, SharePoint, and Windows training solutions and the production of online and printed training resources. For more information about OTSI, visit *www.otsi.com,* or for advance information about upcoming training resources and informative tidbits about technology and publishing, follow us on Facebook at *www.facebook.com/Online.Training.Solutions.Inc.*

Acknowledgments

I am extremely grateful for the unflagging support and contributions of Jaime Odell, Kathy Krause, and Susie Carr at OTSI—this book (and so many others) wouldn't exist without our fabulous team! Thank you also to Rosemary Caperton and Kim Spilker at Microsoft Press, and Laura Norman at Pearson Education, for making the MOS Study Guide series for Office 2016 a reality.

Finally, I am so very grateful for the support of my daughter, Trinity. Her confidence, encouragement, and terrific cooking when I'm working late bring me great joy.

Now that you've read the book...

Tell us what you think!

Was it useful?
Did it teach you what you wanted to learn?
Was there room for improvement?

Let us know at https://aka.ms/tellpress

Your feedback goes directly to the staff at Microsoft Press,
and we read every one of your responses. Thanks in advance!

 Microsoft